MODERN TRIBAL POLITICS

Why Liberals Are Liberal
Why Conservatives Are Conservative
Why Capitalism is Superior to Socialism
Why Politicians Lie
How to Restore the Unique American Culture

PERRY JOTTER

NEWMAN SPRINGS PUBLISHING
320 Broad Street
Red Bank, NJ 07701

First originally published by Newman Springs Publishing 2018

ISBN 978-1-64096-602-4 (Paperback)
ISBN 978-1-64096-603-1 (Digital)

Printed in the United States of America

CONTENTS

Section 2: American Culture and Politics

Section 3

PREFACE

The public relations and legislative battles against the classist liberal nanny state are lost. The only hope for not losing the war against liberalism is to open a new front run by the states and with wide public support. An Article V Constitutional Convention is the best, perhaps only, way to avoid the complete de-evolution of our unique American culture into a liberal kleptocracy. Such a convention could address the issues that plague America today. Many of these issues are addressed in this book with suggestions as to how a constitutional convention may help save our unique heritage. Our forefathers committed treason when they pledged "our Lives, our Fortune, and our sacred Honor" to right the wrongs of an overpowering, unrepresentative, unresponsive government. Fortunately, they included the Article V clause in the Constitution to enable the states to peacefully and orderly right the grievous wrongs being done by the very government they established. Nevertheless, wide public support can only be achieved by individuals willing to put their reputations on the line and risk public humiliation, harassment, and retribution by this government and its lackeys. I hope that conservative politicians, the Tea Party, and conservative TV and radio hosts are willing to stand up for freedom and the American way.

In order to understand how and why we are losing our heritage, it is necessary to realize that Homo sapiens is a tribal species. That is, individuals cannot exist by themselves but only as members of tribes. Our social structure and culture is the result of thousands of years of tribal evolution. As a consequence, the first portion of this book concentrates on primitive tribal society and the mechanism of tribal evolution. It makes no difference if the evolutionary time span of tribalism from the first humans to today is 10,000 years or 100,000 or 1,000,000 years. The fact remains that man existed originally in an isolated asocial state with only a few other individuals around, and yet by the time of Christ, humans had discovered fire, farming, herding of animals, money, commerce, and trade, and were organized into numerous tribal societies. There were tribes with different languages, cultures, and traditions—friendly, hostile, good, and evil. It is immaterial to tribal evolution if the origin of man's evil is due to original sin or the struggle of living in a hostile environment. Tribal evolution[1] is the mechanism whereby society evolves. Wikipedia notes that "evolution is an *unguided* process." Accordingly, tribal societies can and have evolved to higher levels and de-evolved to lower ones.

This book also argues that modern American liberal leaders advocate a retrograde movement toward a racist, classist society the goal of which is to establish and enrich a ruling class at the expense of the *lower* classes. The methods of the ruling class are inherently self-serving and greedy. They use our primitive insecurity to achieve wealth and power. Liberalism has in the past and always will ultimately lead to violence and chaos.

This book argues that the traditional American culture based on laissez-faire capitalism is the ultimate social organization and is the best approach to a classical liberal society and proposes that limiting congressional compensation to the median income of the people they serve will stop the racist, classist, repressive, liberal, progressive movement and restore the unique American culture.

Over the years, the propaganda arms of the liberal, progressive, socialist, and communist movements have intentionally *redefined* many terms for their political advantage. Paramount among them are liberal and conservative. Throughout this book, the term liberals and liberalism refers to modern American liberalism as embedded in the Democrat party, unless explicitly stated to be classical liberalism.

---

[1] Evolution, as used in this book, refers to the traditional sense of evolution—"the continuous adaptation… to the environment…" Webster's Encyclopedic Unabridged Dictionary of the English Language, 1989.

American liberalism has its roots in the New Deal, the Fair Deal, and the Great Society programs. The major premise of ***American liberalism*** is the establishment of a ***large, all-powerful government*** to redistribute wealth in the hope that it will create equality. American liberalism, or just liberalism, is quite distinct from ***classical liberalism*** which advocates civil liberties and political freedom with a ***limited government*** under the rule of law.

Capitalism refers to laissez-faire capitalism which is based on the ***private ownership of property with minimal government regulations to protect civil rights, property rights, and the production of a fair profit on investments***. The terms modern capitalism, conservative capitalism, and free market capitalism are used interchangeably to describe various facets of capitalism. The class-based European capitalism of the nineteenth century and liberal crony capitalism against which Marx and Engels railed against are explicitly not included in the term *capitalism* as used in this book.

This book is divided into three sections. The first section is a discussion of man's historical tribal nature and how that influences today's society and politics. It is designed to explain how we got to where we are today, starting from the primitive tribal organization of 5,000; 50,000; or 100,000 years ago through the beginnings of civilization, the last 2,000 years, and, finally, the last one hundred years. The second section is a collection of short essays on the current state of American politics. The second section is designed to briefly address various current issues. There may appear to be some repetition. The intent is to briefly explore the issues' various facets. The third section suggests what needs to be done to move American and world civilization forward for the next one hundred to 1,000 years and how to do it.

POLITICAL TRIBALISM

BACKGROUND

Over thousands of generations, Homo sapiens have evolved in a tribal environment controlled by two sets of competing instincts and emotions. On the one hand are the selfish, greedy instincts for individual survival, and on the other are the sharing, magnanimous, altruistic instincts for group survival. This system of instincts evolved in a small tribal environment where everyone knew everyone's needs and capabilities and personal interactions were determined accordingly. But there was one set of instincts for intra-tribal interactions and a different set for inter-tribal situations. The intra-tribal instincts determined the culture of a tribe. The inter-tribal instincts determined the domination of some cultures over others.

Over the last 5,000 years, with the development of agriculture and other technological advances, a hierarchical class-based system evolved. The class-based system established the needs and responsibilities of the different classes; in effect, governing the interactions between individuals in large populations. In a class system, the personal contact of the small tribe is lost between classes, and each class in itself becomes a tribe. As a result, the inter-tribal instincts control the interactions between individuals of different classes, while the intra-tribal group survival instincts dominate within classes. One result is that since there is no restraint on the selfish instincts between classes, the basic instinct for survival of individuals in the dominating *higher* classes is to seize and maintain control over the lower *subservient* classes. This control relies on the propensity of people to trade their freedom for security.

Over the last 500 years, a new system for the peaceful interaction of large populations has evolved. In the seventeenth century, Hobbes, Locke, and Rousseau observed that individual happiness was most easily achieved in small (a few hundred), free, democratic organizations based on social contracts, and that people will naturally organize themselves into these tribal groups. Larger populations can be organized into numerous small dynamic tribes where individuals are free to join as many or as few tribes as they wish. These tribes act like individuals and use the altruistic instincts in an intra-tribal way and the selfish instincts in an inter-tribal way.

An important recent advance in civilization is the realization that resources are not finite. There is no need for tribes to fight over the distribution of resources as free enterprise can produce more resources *on demand*. In the process of generating and distributing the resources, businesses provide their employees the security formerly provided by the *upper* classes. But employees have the freedom to switch employers or start new businesses. All organizations such as churches, social organizations, charities, and businesses which serve the people best and do the most good survive and evolve; those which do not, die.

This section attempts to explain how and why the basic instincts of the primitive tribal structure are the foundation of the two current competing political cultural organizations—socialism and conservatism. It speculates about how modern technological developments may influence the competition and what we, as individuals, can do to influence the outcome.

INTRODUCTION

Historically, all reactionary forces on the verge of extinction invariably conduct a last desperate struggle against the revolutionary forces, and some revolutionary forces are apt to be deluded for a time by this phenomenon of outward strength but inner weakness, failing to grasp the essential fact that the enemy is nearing extinction while they themselves are approaching victory.[2]

—Mao Tse-tung

We are in the midst of an epic battle in a conflict that has gone on not simply for centuries but since the beginning of mankind—a conflict of tribal cultures. The battle is between the old class-based authoritarian cultures of Europe—the *reactionary forces*—and the new North American egalitarian, hard work- and freedom-based culture—*the revolutionary forces*—where all men are created equal and their future is based primarily on their ability and hard work. Because the time frame of this tribal battle is multigenerational, we tend not to see the ebb and flow of the warring tribal cultures. But our being, our happiness, our existence, our destiny, and the hap-

---

[2] Mao's use of *reactionary forces* broadly refers to the traditional classist societies of the West and *revolutionary forces* as communism, socialism, and liberalism. However, it is the thesis of this book that the reverse is true—that socialism and liberalism are the old reactionary forces and that American capitalism is the revolutionary force. Indeed, this revolutionary capitalistic force is *approaching victory* in China today, while the liberals in America are conducting a desperate struggle against the conservatives.

piness and destiny of our children are controlled by the outcome of this battle.

Every day, our tribal instincts influence how we react socially and politically to the world around us. Tribalism can explain why a liberal is liberal, why a conservative is conservative, why political propaganda is more effective than political persuasion, and why the American culture is unique. Most of today's cultural, political, and personal issues can be understood and explained from the view point that the tribe is the living entity and tribal culture is the personality. We, as individuals, are merely one of the pieces of the tribe. The cells of our body live, reproduce, and die, but it is the entire body that lives on. We are the cells, the tribe is the body, the culture the species. The resolution of the cultural conflict will determine the future of the American species.

This section is about tribal evolution and survival of the fittest. What is a tribe? How did our small tribal instincts evolve? How do instincts govern tribes? Do the same instincts that work well for small tribes with about 200 individuals work well for large tribes with over 20,000,000,000 individuals? Can instinctual behavior be changed?

To understand these concepts, an explanation of what a tribe is and how tribal intelligence and tribal communication operate is needed. Some issues such as morality, warfare, or politics can be easily understood, but others such as the distinction between instinctual and reasoned behavior need a more detailed explanation.

Disclaimer: This book is my interpretation of modern political society based on readings in many overlapping technical and social science areas. This work is intended to present the big picture, *with general concepts for a general audience. Therefore, general, intuitive terms and concepts are often used instead of the more technical terms and specific concepts such as evolutionary biology, group selection, sociocultural evolution, and modeling.* [3,4]

---

[3] Group selection refers to the idea that genes evolve in a tribe or culture because of the benefits they bestow on the group as a whole.

[4] Sociocultural evolution involves cultural and social evolution. Sociocultural modeling describes how and why cultures and societies change over time.

For example, this work uses tribe, inter-tribal, intra-tribal *instead of* group, between group, *and* within group *respectively. This is because the behaviors and instincts that formed the cultures that control our everyday lives evolved predominately when the tribe was the only social organization. In addition, the term* selfish instincts *is used to collectively describe the human behaviors which are for the exclusive benefit of oneself. Examples of these behaviors are: greed, gluttony, hoarding, laziness, etc. They evolved out of a fear of hunger, sickness, or loneliness (homelessness). Conversely, the term* altruistic instincts *is used for all characteristics that benefit other individuals or the tribe as a whole. For example, some altruistic instincts are sharing, compassion, empathy, helping the sick and elderly, etc.*

The interested reader is encouraged to explore all of these topics in more detail via the references, the literature, and the Web.

TRIBALISM

In their book *The View from the Center of the Universe*, cosmologist Joel Primack and his wife Nancy Abrams argue that the universe was made for human beings. "Much smaller creatures than we are could not develop the complexity necessary for intelligence; much larger ones would be limited by the time it takes information to travel across their brains."[5] But the true ultimate beings for which the universe was made are tribes. Tribes of people are capable of much greater collective intelligence, accomplishments, and a much wider range of collective personalities (i.e., cultures) than isolated individuals. It is tribalism, tribal communication, and tribal intelligence that make Homo sapiens unique.

Although we share a very large percentage of our genetic makeup with other higher forms of life, they do not have the combination of sophisticated communication, varied intelligence, and group organization that has allowed human beings to dominate the world. Tribalism is at the center of our achievements. Sending a man to the moon could not have been done by a single human being; it took a tribe of human beings. We are a tribal species. The unit of human evolution is not the individual, but the tribe.[6] To understand

---

[5] Jerry Adler. "Finding a Home in the Cosmos." *Smithsonian*, July 2006, p. 72–74.

[6] It is popular to talk of a *village* as the basic unit of society, but a *tribe* is more accurate. A *village* implies a group of houses or permanent shelters at a physical location and the people associated with them. A *tribe* connotes a group of people with or without permanent shelters. Over many years of social evolution, it can be argued that permanent *villages* are a recent development of the last

this, first we must define what a tribe is, then examine the nature of tribes.

A traditional tribe is a small group of people living as a single entity. That is, the group, not any one individual in the group, is responsible for the group's basic needs—food, water, shelter, protection from predators, etc. The tribe collectively obtains food, water, and shelter. Consider food. If one individual in the tribe obtains food, he must share it with everyone. That is, food belongs to the entire tribe, not the individual. Shelter, in the form of caves or villages, is for the entire tribe, not isolated individuals. Tribes do not select living sites that are not suitable for every member. It is detrimental to the tribe if some individuals are forced to live in exposed, unsafe places while others live in absolute security.

Tribes are, of course, the most primitive form of Homo sapiens' social organizations. All social groupings share certain characteristics. They have a common method of communication. They have a type of group intelligence. Members of social organizations have two sets of instincts: individual selfish instincts and intragroup altruistic instincts. The first more primitive, selfish set of human instincts was developed during pre-tribal evolution for self-preservation and reproduction. The second altruistic set evolved as a necessary condition for the creation, preservation, and propagation of tribes.

Our early ancestors lived in hunter-gatherer social organizations for millennia during which time our basic selfish instincts were established and refined by the forces of evolution. During this pre-tribal era, culture was simple. It was based on everyone for himself and the survival of the fittest. Life was hard, and our ancestors were only able to procure food, clothing, and shelter as needed. In this hostile environment, cautionary instincts we would label today as *laziness*, *selfishness*, and *greed* were evolutionary advantages. For example, evolution would favor the *lazy* individuals that instinctively procured no more food than immediately necessary and *greedy* individuals that hoarded the food they did find for themselves and immediate

---

5,000 years or so, while *tribes* have always been and still are the basic unit of the human social structure.

family. These instincts would be an evolutionary advantage because venturing from the safety of a cave or shelter exposed the individuals to danger from the elements, marauding animals, and even other humans. Moreover, since an adult was necessary to raise children, it was to an individual's evolutionary advantage to satisfy their own *selfish* needs first before the needs of their children.

Simple individual evolution favors instinctual, selfish individuals that hoard versus those that share. Altruism toward fellow group members is discouraged by the Darwinian advantage of surviving and having personal offspring. Tribalism requires a mechanism for developing altruistic instincts. Intra-tribal communication was required for individuals and related family members to receive credit for and receive the benefits of an altruistic act. The altruistic act may be sharing a valuable resource, such as food during a shortage. Among the Tchadian Kanembu tribe in Africa, sharing is mandatory.[7] It keeps the tribe alive. Sharing food during hard times is most difficult, but the memory of worse times is always there. The benefit received from these altruistic acts may be the receipt of food at a later date or even the care of a person's children in case of his or her demise.

Some may argue that a husband and wife or a family can exist and procreate by itself. But in a dangerous world, the success rate of species propagation via individual families is less than that of a group. In isolated families, if both parents should perish in an accident or while obtaining food, it is likely all the children will die. If one parent should be killed, the probability of the survival of the children is reduced substantially, but at least some may live to reproduce. But in a group of families, if one or both parents die, friends and relatives will help raise the children. It is clear that groups consisting of families with members that look out for one another will out evolve other groups. Even today, it is common for families to encourage one child to be a doctor, a second a lawyer, etc. so that the family forms a type of complete small tribe. Family members that emigrate to or discover a better environment often encourage and help other family members to accompany them to keep the family tribe together.

---

[7]   Jim Adams. A Letter to the Editor. *Science News*. April 13, 2002, vol. 161, p. 239.

If a family can develop an altruistic relationship with a coterie of close friends that will help when needed, the chances of raising descendants to adulthood are greatly increased.[8] Neanderthals lived in extended families of ten to fifteen, counting children,[9] but a breeding population of at least 250 adults is needed to sustain a species. A coterie of friends—a proto-tribe—was not only an evolutionary advantage but key to Homo sapiens' evolution. Professor Robin Dunbar[10] has noted that there is a correlation between a species' brain size and the size of their social groups. Based on this correlation, it has been estimated that human social groups should be roughly around 150 individuals. Accordingly, this number seems to be the approximate "number of good friends;... the size of hunter-gatherer bands; the population of Neolithic villages; and the strength of army units."[11] Obviously, 150 is less than the 250 needed to sustain a population. First of all, both numbers are very approximate. More importantly, humans are capable of handling much larger amounts of information by grouping then into *chunks*, so that groups with over 600 individuals are easily attainable. For example, 150 females, 150 males, 150 children, and 150 individuals from related tribes. Over time, group selection would produce tribes and even new races with the altruistic genes based on *small* tribal groupings.

Altruism is normally thought of as an act between individuals, but there is tribal altruism also: altruism toward the entire tribe. Many people have an inherent need to contribute to society—a feeling of worthiness. These instincts are due to the tribal need to procreate. That is, a tribal culture multiplies by increasing possessions and resources which allow the expansion of its population. When the population increases to a size too big for the small tribe environment, conflict arises and the tribe divides.

---

[8] "Female baboons who forged close ties to kin and community members... raised substantially more than their share of infants to at least age 1." from "Baboons demonstrate social proficiency." *Science News*. December 20 & 27, 2003 vol. 164, p. 397.

[9] Joe Alper. "Rethinking Neanderthals," *Smithsonian*, June 2003, pp. 83–87.

[10] Institute of Social & Cultural Anthropology, University of Oxford.

[11] Matt Ridley. "Mind & Matter." *The Wall Street Journal*, February 12, 2011.

Contributing to society can be achieved in many different ways—producing a resource, generating a new idea or invention, dissemination of a valuable discovery, or helping older or needy people. Altruism and the need to contribute are important attributes of a tribe which can be spread by group selection.

Group selection is the process by which tribes evolve. Some scientists are skeptical of group selection. They claim that a very compelling reason is necessary to justify group selection.[12] Group selection can happen only if the result is extraordinary in some way, producing a resource that is very valuable. It could be a particular gene that promotes cooperative behavior, altruism, or the division of labor that confers superiority of one group over other groups.[13] Effective, sophisticated intra-tribal communication and collective tribal intelligence are two valuable group resources that would promote tribal based group selection for humans as a superior evolutionary life form.

It has been proposed that "Human cultural diversity can be understood by thinking of different cultures as if they were distinct biological species."[14] An attribute of a species is that the members possess one or more common distinctive characteristics and, most importantly, they interbreed and reproduce those characteristics in their offspring.[15] It is widely accepted that people select mates on the basis of complementing their genes to produce the best gene set for their children. Group selection would support the concept that people also select for the gene set for the entire tribe. That is, when people select a mate, they select one that possesses the set of genes that promotes tribalism, as well as healthy children. Different gene sets produce different tribes with different personalities expressed as the tribal culture. According to the theory of *kin selection*, altruists

---

[12] Richard Conniff, "The Discover Interview," *Discover*, June 2006, p. 58–61.

[13] The FOXP2 gene which is thought to be critical for the development of speech may be such a gene.

[14] As early as the fourteenth century, Ibn Khaldun observed that societies (i.e. tribes) are living organisms that are born, grow and die. More recently Drs. Pagel and Mace expand the concept to cultures in "Behaviorist Seeks What Divides Us," *Discover*, May 2005, p. 20.

[15] *Webster's New Collegiate Dictionary*, 1956.

that do not pass their genes on directly are more than compensated via the reproductive success of their relatives. Thus, culture is the species and the tribe is the individual. A tribal species is a group of tribes with a common culture. The tribe, not the individual, is the unit of evolution. The tribe is a *superorganism.*

Homo sapiens' tribalism has evolved through several stages separated by fundamental events—evolutionary pinches, changes in the brain, physiological changes that enabled speech, etc. The hunter-gather society evolved for hundreds of generations, then about 50,000 years ago, something happened to the human brain. This event allowed the development of speech and language. Then again about 10,000 to 15,000 years ago,[16] a second event occurred that allowed man to *think*, innovate, and make technological advances. These two events may have been separated by a considerable amount of time in human years, but they occurred closely enough in tribal evolution time to be considered simultaneous. This *tribal event* was critical to the development of modern tribalism. When this event occurred and the number of event components is contested. The point here is that at some point(s) in human history, fundamental changes occurred that allowed the present tribal cultures to evolve from the pre-tribal society.

The primitive pre-tribal environment was difficult and security in the form of shelter, food, and protection from outside threats was paramount. Pre-tribal individuals had little social pressure and were free to do whatever they wanted. However, this freedom was not *free*. It was dominated by the need to procure and secure food, shelter, and other necessities. If they did not hunt, they did not eat. But hunting and searching for food was dangerous and was the reason for the evolution of the lazy, selfish, and hoarding instincts that can still be observed in most animals. Nevertheless, pre-tribal individuals evolved the realization that in spite of their instincts to do as little as possible to minimize their exposure to the outside threats, they had the responsibility to provide for their own and their families' needs. If they did not satisfy these needs, no one else would. The responsi-

---

[16] R. G. Klein. "Whither the Neanderthals." *Science*, vol. 299. March 7, 2003, p. 1526.

bility to procure their own food and the freedom to do so however they wanted were the dominant factors in forming pre-tribal society.

A first step for proto-humans to become humans was the establishment of the tribe as the unit of human life, culture, and society by the addition of altruistic instincts to control the selfish pre-tribal instincts. The pre-tribal period lasted many generations and was when all of our primitive personal selfish instincts evolved. During this period, the environment consisted of small, relatively isolated proto-tribes, and conflict was primarily with nature and other proto-tribes.

The transition from pre-tribal individualism to proto-tribal groups to obtain food, shelter, and security required cooperation among tribal members and a mechanism such as social pressure to enforce and promote it. If the proto-tribe was to become a tribe and a useful cultural entity, the welfare of the tribe had to come first. Group selection selected those tribes with individuals that developed an instinct to look out for the welfare of others in the tribe. It was important that every individual looked out for everyone else and that every individual participated equally in tribal activities according to their ability. Whenever there was a successful hunt or a fruitful windfall was found, social pressure and tribal instinct demanded that it be shared with others in the tribe on the assurance that the favor would be returned in kind, in spite of the persistent pre-tribal lazy, selfish, and hoarding instincts. This required the development of trust in your fellow tribal members to fulfill what Hobbes would consider a social contract. Thus, over generations, the individual selfish instincts were augmented with the altruistic instincts that promoted tribalism, but the augmentation restricted individual freedom and reduced the need for individual responsibility.

Small tribal units of no more than several hundred individuals were critical to the integration of the altruistic and selfish instincts. In these small tribes, everyone knew everyone else and their needs and desires could easily be determined by and communicated to other members of the tribe. This was of great advantage when tragedy or sickness struck an individual, but it also ensured everyone contributed according to their ability. Individuals were expected to share whatever they had with others who needed it. Individuals were expected to procure or produce their share of food for the tribe. Individuals were expected to help find and construct shelter. Individuals were expected to sacrifice their freedom and even themselves for the tribe, if necessary. In return, an individual's responsibility was lessened because, if they were a tribal member in good standing, the tribe would provide food and shelter for them and their family when needed. It would provide protection from the outside world. It would do so even if they were incapacitated and incapable of helping themselves. But if it was perceived that they were not contributing to their full potential, they could be censored, rejected, or abandoned. The fear of being outcast from the tribe and losing tribal security and companionship assured that everyone worked up to their ability and adhered to tribal customs and taboos.

The selfish instincts and responsibilities and the freedom to pursue them were and still are a dominant force in our society, but these forces are largely controlled within a tribe by the altruistic instincts. The selfish instincts are a primitive dominant characteristic of survival and are centered in the older more primitive parts of our brain. Because they are so important to survival, they were sublimated to the tribal level. That is, since tribes are living, evolving beings, they possess the same basic needs, instincts, and emotions as individuals to successfully reproduce and evolve. Tribes need food and shelter. Tribes are selfish. Tribes are territorial. Tribes are amoral. Tribes have instincts. Tribes can reason. They possess a *tribe versus the world, nature, and other tribes* instinct. The tribe versus other tribe instinct is recognized today as racism. That is, there is an inherent bias against those that are from a tribe that is different from ours. There is the constant fear that a stranger is intent on taking some of our resources or doing us harm.

Tribes are living amoral beings. They have the freedom, the responsibility to take any action for self-defense or self-promotion. For example, tribes readily engage in warfare with other competing tribes to defend and expand their territory and obtain resources they deem necessary. Tribes respond to Darwin's law of the survival of the fittest. Any action that betters the position of the tribe over competing tribes is allowable, even laudable. Indeed, those tribes that use lying, cheating, threat, and violence most effectively frequently dominate. By expanding, growing, and multiplying, successful tribes reproduce at the expense of lesser tribes.

After the first pre-tribal stage of human evolution, the second hunter-gatherer stage saw the development of small *primitive* tribes as the altruistic instincts developed via group evolution. The third or modern tribal period was from the beginning of civilization (i.e., agriculture) to written history and the industrial revolution. This period was characterized by the beginning of technology and complex communication. Many of the tribal instincts and structures we possess today evolved during this period in response to these developments. The fourth period is from the late industrial revolution to the present and is characterized by exponentially advancing technology, especially communication technologies. This fourth period has developed quickly in tribal evolutionary terms: too quickly for new, accommodating tribal instincts to have completely evolved along with it. Homo sapiens are currently in the process of developing the social instincts and intelligence needed to deal with the new environment created by these advancements.

The class-based *governing* techniques that evolved during the third stage of tribal development are not adequate for a world populated with billions of people. They largely evolved in a hostile environment with ruling classes stealing land and resources from one another and the lower classes, often by force. This system of government resulted in the catastrophic world wars. Our current liberal national government has developed along this model and has resulted in a corrupt political class that has sponsored numerous wars. The smaller state governments have been able to preserve the second period altruistic tribal characteristics and have adapted to the new environment quicker. By and large, they have been able to provide essential services much more effectively and efficiently than the national government. Constitutional modifications are needed to protect the smaller local governments from a powerful, domineering, corrupt national government.

Human Intelligence

Mimicry is one of the elementary components of intelligence. Mimicking, which is copying or following a pattern, a model, or an example, is an inherent component of learning in animals. Mimicry involves pattern recognition and is the ability to recognize spatial or temporal sequences of patterns and predict what the next, previous, or missing pattern is. In mimicry, the cause-effect relationship is deduced. The advantage of performing the action and therefore achieving a desired result is *understood*. Mimicry is how kittens learn to hunt from their mothers. *Smart* animals are capable of learning by mimicry, as when an animal *learns* how to open a door or gate by observation. Mimicry is one method by which people pass down laws and taboos to younger generations. When youth recognize patterns and copy or mimic the actions of elders, the customs and laws become instinct and intuition—the most primitive components of inherited intelligence.

Evolution encodes simple, successful copied behavior as an instinct or intuition. *Instinct* is defined in the dictionary as "behavior that is mediated by reactions below the conscious level"[17] or "a natural and unreasoning prompting to action."[18] *Intuition* is used to describe "thoughts and preferences that come to mind quickly and without much reflection."[19] The reflexive system encodes intuitions in the regions of the brain that produce quick emotional responses based

---

[17] www.merriam-webster.com

[18] *Webster's New Collegiate Dictionary*, 1956.

[19] D. Kahneman. "A Perspective on Judgment and Choice." *American Psychologist*, 58(9), p. 697, 2003.

not on explicit reasoning but on statistical associations. Intuitions are slow to form, but once formed, they are long-lasting.

More formally, instinctual behavior is that which occurs automatically to a set of stimuli. Instinctual behavior is centered in the amygdala—a primitive portion of the mind. Instinctual behavior does not involve any thinking. Automatic instinctual actions are learned when the brain associates a certain triggering situation with a decision as if it were receiving an emotional input. There is not a flood of hormones, as there is with emotions, but there is a sense of what the body would feel like if it were in an emotional state such as stress.[20] Since it is an unthinking action, we are often not aware of it, but many of our everyday actions are controlled by instinct.

Instinct is often confused with emotion. Emotion is a strong feeling; for example, fear, anger, disgust, grief, joy, or surprise. Instinct is natural and unreasoning prompting to action. Instinct can include emotional responses, but instinct does not require strong feeling, only *unreasoning* prompting to action. No thinking is involved in instinctual responses whether emotional or not. "The experience of danger follows two pathways in the brain: one conscious and rational, the other unconscious and innate. The key difference between the two paths is data transmission time."[21] The conscious pathway may take a few seconds; the unconscious pathway can respond within a fraction of a second. The second instinctual, unconscious pathway was critical to survival in the early hostile environment in which we evolved, and thus instinct is a powerful force in intelligence and is still quite powerful today.

Most of our actions are governed by the instincts that evolved in pre-tribal and tribal environments. As a result, humans today have two sets of instincts. One set consisting of selfish, self-interest instincts which evolved during our primitive development—the need for food, shelter, and reproduction and the freedom to procure them. The second set, the altruistic tribal cultural instincts, is contrary to

---

[20] Steven Johnson, "The Theory of Thinking Faster and Faster." *Discover*, May 2004, p.45–49.

[21] "Negative Emotions." *Discover.* March 2003, p. 37.

the self-interest set. Sharing, compassion, and empathy, for example, do not improve one's chances to exist in a cruel world but in fact decrease them. Since the cultural instincts are self-detrimental, we view them as magnanimous for individuals. But in reality, they are basic and essential for tribal survival and evolution. The self-interest set of instincts are still present, and while the altruistic instincts control them in an intra-tribal environment, they are dominant in inter-tribal relationships. The altruistic cultural instincts in individuals are reinforced by a sense of belonging and social interconnectedness. Those groups that do not possess the dichotomy of selfish and altruistic instincts cannot compete against those that do.

Intelligence includes the ability to think and reason new responses to new situations and events. But old instincts are hard to unlearn. "Because the fear response can play a direct role in life-and-death struggles, it's not surprising to find that the brain contains elaborate machinery dedicated to its routines. The fact that the amygdala's basic architecture reappears in so many species is testimony to its evolutionary importance… No matter how calculating and erudite the neocortex (the thinking part of the brain) becomes, it can't simply switch off the amygdala."[22] As a result, there is a constant battle between *thinking* and instinctual behavior.

Societal advancement required a more sophisticated type of intelligence than simple instinct. The *tribal event* spurred the development of the neocortex which is involved with conscious thought, reasoning, and language. Reasoning is the ability to link together chains of patterns from cause to effect. Thinking requires reasoning, judgment, conception, and/or inference. Thinking is the ability to question and analyze which set of matched patterns is best, and select it. Animals do not think the way humans do. "The psychological abilities that make human culture possible are almost entirely lacking in any other species."[23] Thoughtful behavior is that which occurs when several conflicting behaviors are activated and a decision based on the relative merits of the outcome must be made as

---

[22] "Negative Emotions." *Discover*. March 2003, p. 39.
[23] Clive D. Wynne. *Do Animals Think?* Princeton University Press, 2004.

to which action to take. The thinking part of the brain is making progress over the instinctual selfish part by continuing to develop the altruistic instincts. Thinking can achieve in a few years the same behavior which the primitive instinctual evolutionary path takes many generations to produce.

Much of traditional human intelligence is based on unthinking instincts that were developed and honed over the centuries for the individual and small tribe environment. But big tribe and mega-tribe societal environments require *thinking*, whereby decisions are based on the relative merits of the outcome not for the individual or local tribe but for the entire mega-tribe. The Constitution needs to be updated to encourage politicians to use intelligent *thinking* to make decisions that are best for the nation instead of self-serving instinctual decisions.

TRIBAL INTELLIGENCE

Human tribes are the means by which culture evolves and is propagated, and thus are the basis of all civilization. It is not individual intelligence or tool making or communication alone that makes humans unique. It is these features plus our tribal social structure that distinguishes us from the other great apes.[24] These features enable tribal learning and tribal intelligence—an important aspect of the *tribal event* is the development of tribal intelligence.

It is generally agreed that it is intelligence that separates humans from animals. One problem is that no one knows exactly what intelligence is. Or perhaps more accurately, there are many types of intelligence and it is difficult to identify which type or types are critical for being human. Photographic intelligence is the ability to echo back anything seen or heard with or without understanding it. Remembering previous experiences is another type of intelligence. The ability to identify and recognize patterns is a critical intelligence. In addition to these intelligences, there are organizational, leadership, persuasive (communicative), reasoning, scientific, technological, social, medical, warfare, and leadership intelligences, to name but a few. All types of intelligence, collectively, with a sophisticated language to disseminate them, form the basis of tribal intelligence.

Taboos are a type of tribal intelligence that are passed from generation to generation. A taboo or law learned in one generation

---

[24] We share 98 percent of our genes with Bonobos—pygmy chimps. We differ by 1.2percent in terms of single nucleotide changes but by 2.7 percent counting duplications and rearrangements of larger DNA stretches. Charles Q. Choi, "Relative Distance," *Scientific American*, November 2005, p. 36.

can persist in the tribe for many generations, and ultimately perhaps become a common characteristic of a culture. Taboos are for the benefit of the tribe, not the individual. Just as a wolf may chew off a paw caught in a trap to survive even though it is a very important body part, the tribal laws may require some individual sacrifice to save the remainder of the tribe. For example, primitive tribes often kill deformed babies. The baby must be sacrificed for the genetic health of the tribe. Taboos are often passed on by the older *wise men* of the tribe who act as a type of living library of knowledge.

If the tribal laws and taboos are invalid or do not recognize a critical situation, not only may some members of the tribe perish but the entire tribe. Thus, these taboos, customs, and tribal laws—the tribal culture—determine the fate of the tribe as a living entity. Tribes with a poor, stagnant culture will perish at the expense of dynamic evolving tribes. Evolution requires tribes to develop and adopt new ideas and methods (i.e., technology to deal with current problems; to learn).

Instincts, while an *automatic response to a stimulus pattern*, can be learned.[25] Moreover, they can be passed on over the generations by tribes and become a type of the learned tribal intelligence. Whether the behavior itself is encoded in the gene set of the tribe or the behavior is taught by example or communicated by language, instinct is an *unthinking* prompting to action due to some external stimulus. After generations of evolution, *positive* behavior becomes instinctual by the *reflexive system* in the brain.[26]

The term tribal intelligence reflects the fact that a tribe, as a living entity, has more intelligence than any individual in it. Its intelligence is equal to the sum of the intelligence of all of its members. Tribal intelligence is the combination of individual human intelligence and the ability to effectively share or communicate the knowledge within the tribe.[27] We tend to think of the human race as con-

---

[25] This is a more general dictionary sense of instinct rather than the strict scientific *unlearned and inherited* definition.

[26] Carl Zimmer, *Scientific American*, November 2005, p. 93–101.

[27] The significance of a sophisticated language is addressed in the section on Tribal Communication.

sisting of individuals with *average* intelligence, but individuals vary widely in their intelligence.

For each type of intelligence in a tribe, there will be a few individuals with exceptional intelligence, most with normal or average intelligence and a few with below average intelligence.[28] But if the individuals with exceptional and above average intelligence can effectively communicate their knowledge to all the other members of the tribe, then the tribe, as a whole, is as intelligent as the most exceptional individuals. Moreover, since there are individuals in a tribe that are exceptional in all the different types of intelligence, the tribal intelligence is exceptional in all areas.[29]

Tribal intelligence is a tremendous evolutionary advantage. If any of the *tribal events* were due to extreme environmental pressure such as an extended worldwide drought, the tribe with the smartest tribal intelligence would have survived at the expense of the others. It has been argued that as few as a thousand individuals would have survived the *tribal event* disaster. It is possible that only those that existed in an intelligent tribal structure were able to survive and propagate their descendants via group evolution.

But in order for the collective tribal intelligence to be effective, there needs to be leadership. As times change, taboos, laws, and reactions to situations must be reinterpreted and changed. This task falls on tribal elders and leaders. Because there are many different types of leadership intelligence, there are many different types of leaders for different situations. An effective tribe depends on utilizing all

---

[28] Briefly, the intelligence of all of the individuals of a population form a normal distribution with a few individuals, about 4.7 percent, with exceptional intelligence (the lower and upper third standard deviations), about 27 percent, with below and above average intelligence (the lower and upper second standard deviations), and most, about 68 percent with normal or average intelligence (the first standard deviations). There is another .15 percent of brilliant individuals such as Einstein in the population above the third standard deviation. Richard J. Herrnstein and Charles Murray. *The Bell Curve: Intelligence and Class Structure in American Life*. A Free Press Paperbacks Book, 1994.

[29] This does not mean that all tribes act intelligently. Intelligence does not address emotions, etc. A mob is an example of a *tribe* that does not act intelligently.

the different types of intelligent leadership as needed in a dynamic manner.

Tribal intelligence is one of the most important characteristics of Homo sapiens. The current class-based political system is biased toward liberal political intelligence with the trend toward ignoring even denigrating other types of intelligence. For example, religion is a universal tribal intelligence. Our founders recognized that religion is a critical part of tribal intelligence so they instituted the free exercise of all religions without any governmental infringement. The government should be prevented from imposing restrictions on any form of tribal intelligence—religious, economic, scientific, or political.

Two areas of current tribal debate are *climate change* and *evolution versus creation*. The liberal components of the national government are attempting to sway tribal intelligence by providing funding that supports one side of the argument and passing laws that denigrates the other. Since tribal intelligence can only be expanded with the free and open exchange of ideas, the *free speech* and *free exercise of religion* aspects of the Constitution should be reinforced and expanded to prevent the national government from being involved in debates involving tribal intelligence.

TRIBAL COMMUNICATION

As tribes grew from a few individuals to larger groups, it became harder to perceive wants and needs directly and a more effective form of communication was needed to allow members of tribes to express their desires and facilitate cooperation among tribal members. About 40,000 to 50,000 years ago, the human physiology changed in such a way that allowed the development of sophisticated speech and language. Tribes that developed language had a distinct evolutionary advantage. Language allowed individuals to express their needs and desires more openly and to a wider audience, thus providing a more efficient tribal structure.

One of the primary evolutionary advantages of language is that it allows humans to pass on knowledge and instincts without directly experiencing the triggering event. That is, being told (perhaps, repeatedly) of a danger and its consequences has the same effect as experiencing it directly. For example, it is not necessary to experience a snake bite to perceive the danger. We are constantly told to be wary of spiders and snakes, and we develop an instinctual fear of the danger directly without ever actually being harmed. In the same way, the powerful communication ability of language allows tribal rules and taboos to be passed down from generation to generation as a form of tribal intelligence.

The cells of our bodies communicate electronically and chemically. The size of our bodies is determined to some extent by the effectiveness of this communication. The feeling of intense heat on our hand is of limited use if it takes several seconds for the message to travel to the brain and the jerk response to travel back. Similarly, a tribe must be sufficiently large to be self-sustaining, but sufficiently small for efficient intra-tribal communication. Too large a tribe prevents the desires of the individuals from reaching those that can help. Effective communication allows the needs and desires of everyone to be determined and addressed. It allows the best collective decisions to be made. It provides the *nervous system* necessary for the efficient functioning of the tribe as an entity.

The free expression of ideas from one individual of a tribe to another is critical for social improvements. The Founding Fathers had no idea that future communication would be sent over the airways electronically via email and cell phones. They assumed that personal conversations between individuals were private. Communication via US Mail is assumed to be private. The courts have supported the protection of privacy, but the protection to private communication by any means—personal, email, or cell phone—needs to be clearly defined in the Constitution.

TRIBAL CONSCIOUSNESS

Self-consciousness is recognized as a major milestone in the development of human intelligence. That is, a certain level of sophistication is required to see yourself in a mirror and recognize it as your reflection. It is accepted that the ability to distinguish between *me* and *others* allows complex thought, such as empathy and introspection.[30] Social awareness and tribal consciousness is a critical component of tribal intelligence. Tribal consciousness is the ability to distinguish between members of your tribe and other competing tribes and the ability to apply different instincts accordingly.

Tribal consciousness involves seeing another individual and to recognize them as a member of your tribe or not. And if the individual is a member of your tribe, they are worthy of your help, charity, or empathy. If they are members of competing tribes, they are worthy of caution and perhaps even contempt and hostility. Other social animals such as ants achieve group consciousness by *smell*. Humans do it by sight and sound. Humans recognize members of their tribe by how they look, how they act (mannerisms), how they dress, how they talk (both language and accent), etc. Tribal consciousness is the basis of tribal prejudices, such as racism and classism.

Empathy is not instinctive. It is extra-tribal and requires consciousness. We can control empathy. We turn it off when we kill an animal for food. We turn it on when we adopt an animal as a pet. We turn it off when dealing with members of other tribes. We turn it on when dealing with members of our own tribe. In fact, we see

---

[30] B. Bower. "All about Me." *Science*. Aug. 24, 2002, Vol. 162, p. 118.

members of other tribes as tribal competitors. Being tribal conscious, it is our duty to protect our tribe from competing tribes. Since we have no empathy for other tribes, we can attack and eliminate their members if it is to our benefit with no remorse and indeed even with tribal approval. On an intra-tribal level, some actions, such as killing, are immoral since it is a crime against the tribe. But on an inter-tribal level, killing is, at worst, amoral and is often considered heroic. All behaviors are acceptable if they further the position of the tribe. Decisions such as whether killing is moral (*right*) or not (*wrong*) are often emotional and instinctual. "Moral reasoning is often a post-hoc justification."[31]

The conflict between the selfish and altruistic instincts is often recognized as knowing right from wrong. The distinction is clearer when applied to tribal relationships. Actions that are *right* for inter-tribal situations may be *wrong* for intra-tribal situations, and vice versa. While physical killing is normally not tolerated in society today, it is not uncommon for socialist dictators such as Hitler, Stalin, Pol Pot, and Mao Tse-tung to kill the leaders and members of opposing enemy tribes. But killing is sublimated to an abstract action in capitalistic societies. Physically killing potential customers, whether from a competing tribe or not, is counterproductive and is *wrong*. However, the figurative killing of other competing tribes, whether they be a company, business, or organization, is *encouraged* and is *right*. But the figurative destruction of these competing tribes does no physical harm to any individual. Indeed, as in primitive tribal environments, members of defeated tribes may join the conquering tribes.

Tribal consciousness is often embodied in religious dogma which defines right versus wrong. Most religions have advanced to where killing is wrong, so that politicians have resorted to *killing* by public humiliation via their minions in the press. The First Amendment—the freedom of the press—was intended to foment public and political discussion, not to terminate it. Clarification of the First Amendment and the role of the press and media is essential.

---

[31] Sharon Begley. "Researchers Seek Roots of Morality in Biology, With Intriguing Results." *The Wall Street Journal*, 2004.

TRIBAL EVOLUTION

The tribal organization was and still is very successful. As long as the primitive tribes were small and social interactions remained intimate, all was well. In a smaller tribe where everyone was known by everyone else, individual conflicts could be solved quickly in the light of tribal unity and security. But when a tribe became too large for individuals to know everyone, differences and conflicts would occur that were not as easily resolved and peace would only come when the tribe split into two. Moreover, individual freedom allowed individuals to walk away from the tribes with which they disagreed and join neighboring tribes that were more compatible.

In this way, the tribes multiplied and tribal cultures evolved. Tribes with successful cultures would quickly expand to where all of the available resources were exhausted. The game and other food sources became scarce and inter-tribal competition grew. The tribal-level selfish instincts would take over and the result was tribal warfare. The social instinct of putting the tribe first meant preventing other tribes from poaching your resources to the point of physical harm.

The instinct to protect your tribe and resources and destroy your enemies is still strong. Over the centuries, it has evolved from a local tribal instinct into a class-based instinct. The only way to ameliorate this instinct is to eliminate the class structure of society. Laws that establish a class or bestows benefits or obligations on the basis of social or political class should be made unconstitutional.

EVOLUTION OF CLASSES

About 5,000 years ago, at the dawn of recorded history, society substantially changed to meet the needs of a more populous world. Technology involving farming, domestic animals, metal tools, and even writing allowed more and more control over nature and resulted in extensive population growth and mega-tribes. As the population *exploded*, tribal conflicts transitioned from being primarily with nature to being primarily with other mega-tribes, organized as kingdoms, etc. The result was often violent conflict both within and between tribes. These technological advances were rapid in evolutionary terms. The natural selection process did not have sufficient time for new tribal instincts to evolve to support the mega-tribe society, so existing instincts for small tribes were transformed and adjusted for the much larger mega-tribe. A more rigid, hierarchical structured organization was developed, and the close direct personal communication of the small tribal structure was lost. No longer could everyone know everyone and judge their abilities, skills, and needs directly. As the mega-tribes grew, the informal, functional groups of the early tribes became more static and permanent until the original casual dynamic small tribe groupings evolved into classes.[32]

---

[32] "Hunter-gatherers had neither the means nor the need to create social hierarchies. That process (which entailed the division of labor and the emergence of a managerial caste) got under way only after humans settled down to farm. Once they learned to grow enough food to nourish those not directly involved in its production, it was not far to civilization—broadly defined as a society endowed with government, social classes, urban centers, extensive trade, and widespread

Initially, the groupings were dynamic, being in existence for a few weeks to a few years depending on the need. Individuals could contribute in areas that took advantage of their natural talents. Group membership often overlapped. For example, the warriors and the hunters would be drawn from the same population since they utilized similar skills. In order for the tribe to become a living species, it needed to develop specialized organs—brains, arms, and legs—and nourishing organs in the form of sub-tribes. That is, a portion of the tribe—the chiefs—became the rulers or the brain. Ultimately, the managerial caste. A portion of the tribe—the warriors—became the extremities for defense and offense. A portion became the nourishing organs—the hunters, farmers, and laborers—providing food, clothing, and shelter.

The sub-tribes became more permanent, eventually evolving into classes or castes. Tribes and even sub-tribes became too large to judge individuals based on personal acquaintance. The primitive tribal instincts of family prevailed. Since tribalism evolved from family units in which everyone was known at least casually, when confronted with a larger group, the *natural* evolutionary tribal instinct was to trust the members of your family over strangers. The classes were no longer dynamic but groupings based on family and heredity. Individuals were not judged on their intelligence and ability but on how they dressed and acted and where they were born. The result of classism was a more stable social structure suitable for large tribes with a communication system more advanced than direct verbal and visual contact.

Classism was achieved at a substantial loss of the instinctual tribal freedom and responsibility. The basic freedom and sense of responsibility inherent in small tribes allowed individuals to select how best to serve themselves and their tribe. They were not forced into a role based on their parentage. This functional flexibility is critical in a small tribal community with limited human resources and

cultural influence." Kenneth Miller. "Showdown at the O. K. Corral." *Discover*, September 2005, p. 64.

is present in all primitive tribal structures but is lost in class-based political systems.

The permanent classes allowed tribes to evolve into large social structures or mega-tribes such as city-states, kingdoms, nations, and empires. The advantage of classes for such entities was that the tribal interpersonal relationships of small tribes were no longer necessary. They were still important for small local organizations, but people were able to judge a stranger's needs and service to society based on the stranger's class which could be recognized by a stranger's mannerisms: the way he talked, acted, and dressed. The ruling classes of kings and nobles, the warrior classes of knights and mercenaries, and the working classes of peasants, farmers, and merchants were all easily distinguishable. As permanent class organization became more structured, there were fewer intra-class conflicts.

In a rigid class-structured society, the primitive selfish instincts are not controlled by the social tribal means. More accurately, primitive tribal social forces are only active within sub-tribe classes, not between classes. The openness, freedom, and flexibility between functionaries of a primitive tribe were restricted to members of the same class, while the relationship between classes became equivalent to inter-tribal competition. That is, a peasant farmer cannot tell his lord or a knight how they should behave, and a nobleman cannot tell the royal family how to act. In the hypothetical perfect class-based society, behavior was defined class membership. If an individual violated those behaviors, only members of his class could reprimand him. But due to selfish instincts, it was not uncommon that other members of the class were violating the same rules so they would not criticize each other.

As a result, over the generations, the primitive individual-centric instincts of hoarding, selfishness, and laziness were no longer controlled by social tribal forces and transformed the institution of classes from benefiting the mega tribe to benefiting the individual members of a class. That is, individuals in the classes saw the classes as a means for security and self-preservation—in essence, their own tribe. The *divine right of royalty* is an extreme example of self-preservation of an individual and his family. It is not an obvious advantage to a mega-tribe to be ruled by the same family for many generations when other better qualified individuals are available.

The sub-tribe classes became effective tribes within the mega-tribe. The distinction being that a tribe can and will act in its own self-interest against any other tribe in the mega-tribe and other tribes in an amoral fashion. Previously, members of a sub-tribe acted as a tribe but in cooperation with the other sub-tribes and with the welfare of the parent mega-tribe paramount.

In order to maintain the class structure, a fundamental view of the world had to be changed. In pre mega-tribal times, the resources needed for living, such as food, materials for clothing and shelter, and making tools were assumed to be owned by the tribe and freely available to anyone that needed them. Tribal welfare and individual security were dependent on these resources being readily available to everyone and were defended by the tribe from other tribes. The ruling classes initially defended these resources for the welfare of the mega-tribes but gradually assumed ownership of them for themselves. The *lower* classes (sub-tribes) enjoyed the resources at the discretion of the ruling class. When the resources, such as parcels of land and villages, became too extensive to be controlled by one individual, portions were parceled out to subservient ruling class underlords in exchange for their loyalty. These underlords in turn parceled out the resources to their subclasses. These parcels and the peasants they supported became the sole support for the ruling classes and via the selfish hoarding instinct for something to possess and own. The peasants at the lowest level of the hierarchy accepted the arrangement because the protection their lord promised against the other competing lords appealed to their tribal instinct for security. The entire feudal structure was based on tribal instincts. The nobility had leadership intelligence and a selfish instinct for hoarding. The peasants lacked leadership intelligence but had a selfish instinct for security for which they were willing to give up primitive tribal freedom.

In time, the leadership classes used technology to reinforce and defend their position of dominance and maintain control. Technological innovations initially for peaceful pursuits such as farming and hunting were co-opted by the leadership classes for warfare. At first, tribal leaders used warfare to defend tribal resources from other tribes, but after the transition to kingdom mega-tribes, leaders used it more for gaining and maintaining power and prestige than for the benefit of the *lower* farmer and trader classes. Expansion of the kingdom's territory was often justified as for the benefit of the entire mega-tribe, but frequently it served only for the selfish self-aggrandizement of the ruling class. The history of civilization illustrates that the mega-tribe with the most advanced warfare technology and organizational skills dominated.

Political leaders use classism to gain and maintain control of the masses. We are not Americans, but black Americans, white Americans, Asian-Americans, or Hispanic Americans. Class-based politics, by definition, is based on passing laws to divide the country into antagonistic groups. These laws intentionally or unintentionally severely restrict the freedom to achieve based on one's talents. Class-based laws take away the feeling of self-worth achieved by a person reaching their goals on their own. Classism has no place in the American culture.

Tribal Technology and Communication

Technological advancements started with learning how to build and maintain a fire. The next advances, such as the throwing stick, the atlatl, were slow in coming. Farming, one of the most critical advances, took many years to advance from the digging stick to the hoe to the plow. Some advances such as irrigation and food preservation resulted in extraordinary expansions of land resources. Frequently, subsequent advances in technology were based on the previous. For example, pottery was not invented until there was a need for storing food produced by the advances in food production. As more technology was developed, a larger population could be supported and even more technology developed. Slowly at first, technology spread from tribe to tribe, initially perhaps by mimicry, but sophisticated intra- and inter-tribal communication was a critical component of the spread of technology.

Communication itself has also benefited greatly from technology. Modern speech and language are often cited as a hallmark of modern human beings. From the first clay tablets to the telephone to the internet, technology has increased the speed and extent of communication exponentially over time. With effective modern worldwide communication and worldwide tribal technology and communication, the human tribe only needs one Einstein for the whole world to possess the theory of relativity.

Group evolution is a slow process requiring many generations to shape our instincts. Initially, natural selection was able to keep up with technological advances, but since approximately the beginning of written history, the evolution of tribal instincts began to lag. Today, technology can advance in a few weeks—an amount that would take natural selection many generations to develop the proper instinctual response. Tribal intelligence and tribal communication must augment the role of tribal instincts.

The conflict of the competing evolving cultures is more visible, dynamic, and strident today than ever because of the sophisticated level of modern communication. Since modern democratic decisions and laws are based on public opinion, various groups are using TV, paper, radio, and the Web in a way never before experienced to try to influence our opinions, and thus our laws and society. Tribal intelligence has not had sufficient time to evolve an instinctual response to these new forms of communication. Logic and reasoning must augment tribal intelligence where individuals do not fully understand how these new forms of communication are being used.

Government is perhaps the slowest social institution to evolve, so that the primitive selfish instincts often dominate. Government needs a new breed of politicians that is willing to embrace the changing communication environment to promote logic and reasoning, not for themselves but for the benefit of the nation.

CLASSISM AND WARFARE

<blockquote>

"There was no professional fighting class; every man was his own policeman, every man a soldier on active duty *for his adult life. Each clan had its traditional major enemies, with whom it always fought, and its minor enemies, with whom it was alternately at peace or at war."*[33]

—Said of the primitive tribes of New Guinea's highland when they were first discovered.

</blockquote>

The date of the appearance of inter-tribal warfare is not precisely known but is probably due to contention over amassed resources.[34] In first contact (See insert above), it appears that inter-tribal conflict is *normal*, presumably over limited natural resources such as arable land. But evidence suggests that peace was more desirable in primitive tribes, for while "fighting men… [were] valued for their qualities of confidence, aggression, and fearlessness, there was even greater value placed on the abilities of the reconciler."[35]

Some hypothesize that the warfare instinct is pre-tribal and is due in part to the basic animalistic need to reproduce and spread

---

[33] Bob Connolly & Robin Anderson. *First Contact.* Viking Penguin Inc., New York, 1987, p. 64.

[34] Attributed to Joyce Marcus. University of Michigan Museum of Anthropology-Josie Glausiusz. "It Takes a Village to Raise a Ruckus." *Discover.* Jan. 2004, p. 12.

[35] Bob Connolly & Robin Anderson. *First Contact.* Viking Penguin Inc., New York, 1987, p. 65.

genes. They claim that humans may possess a *rape* gene.[36] Such a gene would be responsible for action similar to that of a male lion when they take over a pride. They kill all of the cubs of a pride and impregnate the lionesses. Tribal taboos control any human *rape* instinct within the traditional small tribe. But during warfare, pillaging and rape is acceptable (perhaps even encouraged), thus spreading the gene.[37] For example, Tatiana Zerjal and Tyler-Smith report that a *distinctive star-cluster chromosome* is found in the human population which corresponds "almost exactly to the extent of Genghis Khan's empire. 'And they hypothesize that the cluster was spread by Genghis Khan.'"[38]

Primitive tribes were primarily hunter-gatherers supplementing their diet with some crops. As farming technology improved, it resulted in an ever expanding population requiring more resources. These larger tribes required a more complex system of social order than primitive tribal instincts and taboos. The result was the rise of a ruling class and, ultimately, classism in general. Over time, the amoral inter-tribal relationships were assumed by the ruling classes not only for the preservation and expansion of the tribe but for the preservation and promotion of their classes and their status.

The upper classes used the traditional tribal laws and instincts to expand and consolidate their power. Over time, the ruling class used the tribal law that resources—land, in particular—belonged to the tribe, not individuals, to take ownership of the land by maintaining that it was for the common good. They used the primitive desire for security to keep order and control of the lower classes. For example, a tenet of feudalism was that the lords were to protect the serfs from competing lords in exchange for their labor on the land. Feudalism is in fact a de-evolution of tribalism.

The evolution of political order is founded on warfare. The ruling classes use the racism instinct—the innate fear of compet-

---

[36] Sharon Begley. "In Explaining How We Got This Way, Beware of the Just-So Story." *The Wall Street Journal*, 2004.

[37] A pre-tribal rape *instinct* is probably too complex to be controlled by a single gene but, nevertheless, the rape instinct may exist and be inherited.

[38] Robert Kunzig. "The Hidden History of Men." *Discover*. Dec. 2004, p. 33– 39.

ing tribes—to justify conflict and warfare with neighboring lords. Warfare is dominant throughout human history and is dominant in our world today.

Historically, technology was not used to create wealth but, with the instinct of hunter gathering, to take wealth from other tribes via military domination and warfare. The history of all *civilized* areas of the world is replete with wars and one kingdom, city-state, or republic fighting with other such entities.[39] In recent history, and even today, there are numerous wars taking place. If tribes are the living beings, then conflict between them is amoral and is a natural, even an essential, part of the evolution of tribal species.

The development of classes allowed the control of large populations (super-tribes) which could support specialists such as scientists and technicians. Selfish, patrimonial ruling classes supported the scientific/technology classes for the development of superior warfare machines to dominate their neighbors and increase their power, prestige, and wealth. Many, if not all, great human inventions were developed for or applied to military applications early on: fire, the wheel, gunpowder, and the computer. Even today, a primary focus of technology is for military applications. Fortunately, many of these developments are useful in everyday life and contribute to the advancement of peaceful civilization.

Warfare is a fundamental tool of class-based societies. As history has shown, in class-based kingdoms, empires, and socialistic societies with dominant ruling classes, violence in the form of riots and war is *justified* as being for the benefit of the society but, ultimately, it is for the acquisition of wealth and power by the ruling classes to satisfy their selfish, greedy instincts. Eliminating the governmental use of classism and racism in laws and edicts will reduce if not eliminate inter- and intra-tribal conflicts and promote world peace.

---

[39] Francis Fukuyama. *The Origins of Political Order: From Prehuman Times to the French Revolution.* Farrar, Straus, and Giroux, 2011.

The Resurgence of Freedom and Private Property

Class-based societies restrict freedom. People are bound to the duties of their inherited class. They are not allowed to move from one class to another, regardless of their talents. As restrictive as the class systems are, they have been quite successful as a whole and support large populations. But the lower classes are, in essence, slaves who exist only to serve the ruling classes. Their needs and desires are not of concern to the ruling classes, except when they might impact their comfort. When there is a disaster such as a crop failure, the peasants and serfs are forced off the land. When there is excess labor in any of the lower classes, the people become a burden and are forced to find work outside their station.

Not just anyone can leave the comfort of their *position in society* as defined by their hereditary class and strike out in a new endeavor. It requires a person with strong primitive, selfish freedom and responsibility instincts and/or dire necessity. The survival instincts are often the initial incentive to try new activities. If and when one is able to sustain one's family, the selfish instincts provided the impetus to obtain and hoard additional resources. The freedom instinct provides the impetus to reject the class strictures that limit goals.

Cottage industries, manufacturing,[40] merchandising, commerce, and trade developed in such circumstances. In class-based societies, merchants and manufacturers are considered a separate class. But in Western European societies, there are no barriers to entering the merchant classes, only barriers to leaving the other classes. Since being a successful merchant or manufacturer is based more on effort and successful enterprise not birth, members of the merchant class are relatively free of restrictive class structures.

The early classes were based predominately on governance, military, agricultural, religious, and scholarly activities. Those individuals that were able to break free of the strict class system could establish tribal relationships that supported the manufacture of desired items, such as pottery, wine, clothing, weaponry, etc. Superior manufactured items were recognized and desired. Trading grew as a consequence of and a necessity for manufacturing technology.

The selfish and hoarding instincts enticed individuals to use the income from their efforts to create more and more resources they could use for trade or possession. This was the beginning of commerce and the beginning of the end of depending on nature to provide an individual's basic wants. Tribal resources were no longer limited to what nature provided. If more or better food was desired, manufacturers would produce and *sell* more products and *buy* the food they desired. Excess resources could be generated by resourceful, hardworking individuals. These resources were shared with the less fortunate within the tribe because of the altruistic tribal instincts. But because these societies were still small village size, the habits of all the individuals were known by all. Those individuals that had a reputation for being lazy were not coddled but required to contribute their fair share of work to the tribe.

Trading has always been a component of tribal society. At first, an expert bow maker might trade a bow for meat or a pot produced by another member. When *new*, better technology, such as the atlatl,

---

[40] *Cottage industries* and *manufacturing* as used here refers to the production of items beyond the needs of the immediate family and tribe and intended to be traded for other goods or services.

long bow, or Damascus steel, was developed or an unusual or *exotic* product, such as spices, silk, and tea, was discovered, the demand for such items and the potential profit was so great that merchants and traders often risked robbery and their lives to obtain and distribute them.

Pre-tribal instincts such as freedom and hoarding supported the concept of property ownership and the right to trade it for something you felt was more valuable: two instincts that are essential for commerce. Initially, natural resources belonged to no one, to everyone, or to the tribe until claimed and consumed by an individual for their own needs. The instinct for owning property grew along with technology and manufacturing. The instinct for private ownership of property had to be developed before the concept of excessive resources could evolve. If an individual produced a product of value that was owned by the tribe and could be taken away with no compensation, there was no incentive to produce more. The instinct for private ownership evolved with the reemergence of the primitive freedom instinct.

Freedom and private property are essential for a successful capitalistic society. Eminent domain was first discussed by Hugo Grotius in 1625, "For the ends of public utility." Few argue with the need for public roads and buildings, but the taking of personal property to give to a politician's cohort for personal gain is not in keeping with the concept of eminent domain and should be out lawed by constitutional mandate if necessary.

American Freedom

> *My country, 'tis of thee,*
> *Sweet land of liberty,*
> *Of thee I sing;*
> *Land where my fathers died,*
> *Land of the pilgrims' pride,*
> *From ev'ry mountainside*
> *Let freedom ring!*
>
> —Samuel Francis Smith

The Declaration of Independence is a statement of independence from class-based governance, ruling classes in general, and the divine right of kings explicitly. It declares that individual freedom and individual rights supersede the old traditional tribal rights. Indeed, it is a declaration that ruling classes have no rights beyond those of every individual. It states that the *pursuit of happiness* is the responsibility of every free individual and, by implication, it is not the responsibility of a ruling class or government. Since security and contentment are the bases of happiness, and property and resources are the bases of security and contentment, property and resources belong to the individual, not the tribe or the ruling class. Freedom is the natural state of affairs present from our most primitive tribal past. Thus, we can only be governed by our consent, not by a self-imposed ruling class. The rejection of the ruling class, the class structure in general, and the reinstatement of freedom, the right to personal responsibility, and the private ownership of property is the hallmark of American culture in western civilization.

Freedom is the most distinguishing feature of the American culture. It defines who we are and its expression is fundamental to the evolution of our culture. Effective utilization of freedom requires individual intelligence and reasoning. Intelligence is defined as the capacity to make choices based on weighing possible consequences. Reasoning is the ability to connect chains of patterns (and/or intelligent decisions) for many levels from cause to effect. These abilities are in addition to the instinctual intelligence of small tribal laws and taboos. They are required to analyze potential new situations before they occur and are essential when making decisions in a free society.

Intelligence and reasoning rely on education. In the primitive traditional tribe, information was passed from one generation to the next by the elders of the tribe. This intelligence was critical for the survival of the tribe in times of stress. The importance of education has been recognized for centuries. In many countries, education was limited to the upper ruling classes so that they could maintain control over the lower classes. In America, both local and national leaders felt the entire population should be educated so that they could make better decisions, both in their private lives and in the public arena. An educated public was felt to be necessary to be successful in the pursuit of happiness and to judiciously select leaders and governors and, most importantly, to preserve the freedom won from the ruling classes.

The whole people must take upon themselves the education of the whole people and be willing to bear the expenses of it. There should not be a district of one mile square, without a school in it, not founded by a charitable individual, but maintained at the public expense of the people themselves (John Adams).[41]

Education is a critical component of freedom in modern tribal societies. Tribal members need to be educated to know how to think and what to do for the benefit of the tribe. As John Adams implied with his mention of districts of only one square mile needing schools,

---

[41] John Adams. "The Works of John Adams, Second President of the United States: With a Life of the Author, Notes and Illustrations." Volume 9, Little, Brown, 1854, p. 540.

he felt it was the duty of the local tribe to educate local citizens. He realized that federal education would be designed to promote federal goals at the expense of local ones.

AMERICAN TRIBALISM

When the early colonists arrived in America, life was a struggle with little food and resources. It was a necessity that everyone work for themselves and for the benefit of the community as a whole. Thomas Hobbes, a seventeenth century philosopher, argued that scarce resources and overpopulation led people to create small, protective communities (i.e., tribes) that are naturally democratic. Hobbes felt that happiness was most easily achieved in small democratic tribal organizations with individual freedom. Hobbes, Lockes, and Rousseau's social compact theories had a significant impact on the democratic movements and the design of government in the American colonies.[42] For example, the Protestant Reformation, which was a major impetus for fleeing Europe for America, included the concepts of freedom and that physical labor has intrinsic value for its own sake (the Protestant ethic). Everyone worked for themselves, and it was felt that you were rewarded in accordance with how hard you worked and how you shared your rewards with those less fortunate.

In early America there was no government. The colonists believed that a compact or common agreement provided a legitimate government. As an example, consider the Mayflower Compact in the Plymouth colony. A government was necessary to protect private property and the efforts of an individual's labor. These compacts among common men formed the basis of American egalitarian democracy. That is, the principle that all citizens, not just the *higher* ruling classes, had an investment in the government and should be

---

[42] John Briggs. "Social Compact Theory." www.ehow.com

part of its legal formation and operation is the basis of American tribalism. This principle was echoed by Abraham Lincoln in the Gettysburg Address: *"Of the people, for the people, and by the people."* The sum of these two influences resulted in the American culture which rejects the establishment of (ruling) classes, emphasizes individual freedom, the need to work, self-sufficiency, responsibility, the concept of private property, and the obligation of charity. The American pioneering spirit is founded on the need to provide for oneself and fellow tribal members and the freedom and responsibility to do it.

Notable about the early social compacts was that they were initiated by small groups of men with a common interest. It was a small tribal structure wherein there were leaders, but the leadership was dynamic and not class-based. Small tribal organizations are still a dominant force in American society today.[43] The principle of free association promotes a dynamic tribal society. We have the opportunity to join many different tribes—our extended family and friends, our work, our religion, our politics, etc. Our tribal associations are dynamic and they change over our lives depending on our needs and desires. They are not limited by our class or the *tribe* into which we were born.

Dynamic tribes are more cohesive than simple arbitrary groups. Americans still retain the instincts, taboos, and customs of our primitive heritage in today's society, and we apply them to our dynamic tribal organizations. Arbitrary groups have no common purpose and no structure—tribes have both. Tribal members have a common cause and allegiance. Tribal members will support other members, share their good fortune, and come to the aid of others in times of need, even in the face of disagreements and minor grudges. The common cause of a tribe may be for economic gain, charity, religion, or simply fun. Membership in these tribes is voluntary so that people may join or leave as they desire. Whether formal or informal such as businesses, political organizations, churches, charitable organizations, bridge clubs, sport clubs, the Friday night poker game, etc.,

---

[43] Seth Godin. "Tribes"—a book about the need for tribal leadership in America today.

these tribes all share the customs, instincts, and rules of the tribal American cultural species.

Even though initial citizenship is determined by birth, citizenship is dynamic. Individuals are free to move from the jurisdiction of one state or local government to that of another, if they find one government less effective or more oppressive. The mass migration from the south to the north in the early nineteen hundreds and the current migration from the northern industrial states to the freer southern states today are examples of this freedom. The one exception to dynamic tribalism is membership in a national government. Membership is almost always conferred by birth and changing one's nationality, while possible, is difficult.

The American tribal organizations function closest to the original tribal environment—everyone knows everyone, looks out for everyone, and can determine the true needs of everyone. The modern technological culture seeks to preserve the benefits of the primitive tribal instincts by emphasizing the personal physical contact aspect of tribalism. Large organizations such as churches are organized into smaller personal parishes and congregations under the guidance of a minor bureaucracy. There is no method of enforcement between the bureaucracy and the parishes or congregations. The relationship is one of freedom and responsibility. The bureaucracy establishes the responsibilities of the congregations. The congregation is free to agree or not, depending on the need of the members. The members are free to agree with the congregation or not. The only enforcement is ostracism—expulsion from the tribe and losing the tribal companionship and security.

American businesses are tribal, also. Companies, like tribes, have a culture and if a company is unsuccessful, the culture inherent in the company dies, just as a tribal culture dies if the tribe disappears. Companies *fight* other companies for resources and customers. Companies tend to have a hierarchical class organization, but leadership is not hereditary. It is not uncommon and is considered laudatory if a person enters a company at the lowest rank (class) and successfully works their way up to the highest.

There are dynamic class structures even in these *small* tribes. Someone is in control but sub-tribes (i.e., committees) are formed to make decisions. But the structure is dynamic, the boss may change, and group and committee membership varies. Even in government, the president, governors, and legislative bodies have limited terms and power is passed from one individual to the next peacefully because class membership is not required or allowed.

The American tribalism of today is vastly different than that of the old primitive tribalism. For example, warfare has been civilized. A football game is nothing more than a form of civilized tribal warfare. In earlier times, the warfare would have been about access to some valuable resources—farm land or hunting ground. Today, the fight is over prestige and ultimately money. The college or university for which the football team is fighting receives alumni contributions and other rewards in proportion to its success. The effect is a remnant of primitive tribalism wherein aggression, even warfare, against other tribes produced *fierce loyalty* to the home tribe and *fear and hatred* of the opposing tribe.[44] Civilized conflict is not restricted to football games and sporting events. Inter-tribal conflicts are present in every aspect of American dynamic tribalism. Even local governments have occasional *civilized* conflicts with each other.

American altruism is a significant addition to the idealistic principles of the social compact. Altruism is the selfless concern for the welfare of others.[45] But the concept of *others* can vary from culture to culture. American altruism is expressed on at least three levels. First, individual altruism is when you help your neighbor or a member of one of your dynamic tribes. Second, tribal altruism is when one or more members of a tribe help members of another tribe. For example, this may take the form of a bridge club collecting money to buy bridge equipment for another less well capitalized bridge club. Third, in the American tribal culture, altruism has been extended to inter-tribal altruism in the form of giving aid from one mega-tribe to other

---

[44] Attributed to David C. Geary. University of Missouri-Columbia-Dan Seligman. "Root, Root for the Home Team." *Forbes.* March 28, 2005, p. 118.

[45] http://en.wikipedia.org/wiki/Altruism

mega-tribes (countries or cultures). It is the basis of the Marshall Plan for rebuilding and creating a strong, free Europe after World War II. It is represented by the massive giving of aid to countries that suffer natural disasters, etc. As with all altruism, this aid is given with no expectation of payoff or return of any kind.

In summary, the early colonists reinstated small tribal environments in the form of small governments, churches, and other social organizations severely restricting the power of the leadership classes. This American tribal culture is characterized by 1) freedom and free association; 2) egalitarianism (i.e., a rejection of a class structure based on inheritance, nationality, race, or any other distinguishing factor); 3) charity and altruism within and across economic classes, races, tribes, and cultures; 4) a *universal* common culture—a melting pot of language and attitudes; 5) the concept that hard work has merit; and 6) the concept that happiness is achieved via freedom and personal responsibility.

The social compact spirit of the unique American culture can be restored by reestablishing states' rights, restoring the duties of the state, local, and regional governments, and reducing the coercion of an overbearing national government.

AMERICAN CAPITALISM

There is no consensus on the precise definition of capitalism. There is, however, little controversy that the private ownership of the means of production, creation of goods, and services for profit are elements of capitalism. Private ownership in capitalism implies the right to control property, including determining how it is used, who uses it, whether to sell or rent it, and the right to the revenue generated by the property. In the analysis of capitalistic systems, economists often emphasize the degree to which government has control over the means of production, the markets of distribution, and property rights. The extent to which different markets are free, as well as the rules defining private property, is a matter of politics. Modern capitalism evolved starting in the late Middle Ages with the rebirth of freedom and the demise of feudalism when merchants and freedmen were allowed to manufacture and sell items and services wanted and needed by others. Capitalism encourages economic growth and the accumulation of wealth. Private wealth is a keystone of capitalism.[46]

Because wealth is a cornerstone of capitalism and the elitist ruling classes of Europe had the money, they dominated capitalism in the nineteenth century. This evil class-based capitalist system that Marx and other socialists railed against then is similar to crony capitalism that liberals want to impose today. These class-based capitalist systems are quite different from the egalitarian capitalism of conservative America.

---

[46] http://en.wikipedia.org/wiki/Capitalism.

Wealth is an abundance of things needed or desired by others. Wealth is often measured in terms of resources and/or possessions both real and virtual. An important aspect of wealth is that it can be converted into material possessions or services needed or desired by the owner. Some primitive tribes have measured wealth in terms of the number, size, and quality of sea shells. The shells have no inherent value, but in these tribes, individuals are willing to trade items of practical value, such as food, tools, and hospitality for them. It is the willingness of others to trade shells for prestige, possessions, or services that make them valuable. Paper money, silver, and gold, like sea shells, have little or no inherent worth. They cannot be eaten or burned or worn to keep warm. However, via tribal custom or instinct, such items are widely recognized as being a major component of wealth.

Wealth in the form of money is a claim on resources, not a consumption of resources. The true resources are the land, office buildings, stores, warehouses, and factories that a person owns and these resources only have value in that other individuals can use them to satisfy a basic need or create more wealth. A *wealthy* person that holds his wealth in cash, a bank CD, or a company's stock is not consuming resources but contributing to the production of resources by providing the capital that can be used to obtain or produce more.

Conservative capitalism sublimates many of the primitive tribal instincts for the good of society. For example, the fighting instinct of tribe against tribe, which is a waste of human lives and resources, is converted to company against company competition resulting in the optimal utilization of resources. That is, the company which wastes resources will not be able to compete with a more efficient company and will eventually go out of business. The tribal company may die, but the individuals in the company will live on to join or form other tribes in the form of a new company, to work for themselves or someone else, producing goods and services, and continuing to contribute to the wealth of society.

Capitalism also sublimates the primitive tribal instinct against individuals of other classes, races, and cultures. In the prehistory period, tribes evolved in an environment of personal physical relationships. A tribe was an extended family. Tribal membership was not optional. You were a member of a tribe by birthright. Outsiders could easily be recognized by their dress, language, culture, and other physical attributes, such as color and stature. Because the primitive tribes were in a constant state of competition and warfare over perceived limited resources, other tribes and strangers were to be feared and hated. Rarely would an adult outsider be accepted as a tribal member. This prejudice was encapsulated into tribal instincts and biases. But if or when an outsider is accepted, the outsider's characteristics are overlooked and accepted. Since successful capitalist tribal organizations must outcompete their opponents, they cannot afford to hold unwarranted prejudices against potential valuable tribal members. The company that produces the best goods at the lowest price wins. Capitalist systems must utilize the best human resources available. Acceptance into a capitalist tribe is based on ability, language skills, or dress, not race.

Capitalism requires a flexible type of tribal organization. Traditional tribal functionality is still needed to provide security and resources, but the nature of these needs has changed. In essence, a company or a business is a tribe. In a technological based capitalistic culture, money is the only resource needed and security is via tribal membership in an organization that procures money. Everyone in a business knows the capabilities of everyone else and works for the common good. There is a common goal of well-being. But a company is a dynamic tribe. People can join and leave a business at any time. Although businesses may be larger than a traditional tribe, technological advances in communication allow near one-to-one contact. Moreover, the efficiencies of tribal closeness is well understood and there is extensive pressure to keep the number of employees as small as possible.

As a dynamic tribal society, capitalism is highly dependent on education. Education has always been an important part of American culture. In order for individuals to make intelligent choices about which tribe(s) to join, they must be educated to understand the advantages and disadvantages of each. Selecting a virtual tribe not only requires direct contact but a high level of background education.

In a modern capitalistic society, businesses and companies contribute to the overall wealth of the society. The desire to *contribute to society* is nothing more than the primitive tribal altruistic instinct. As such, contributing to society can take many forms: philanthropy, education, helping the poor and needy, inventing new items, and even making and distributing items is a form of contributing to the welfare of the society. The capitalistic need to make money can only be achieved if the marketplace and society is served. Those capitalists that serve society better make more money. The creation of wealth and true tribal altruism is achieved most effectively in a free capitalistic society. The rise of technology freed mankind from the limits of nature. Lack of resources is not a problem today. The efficient manufacture and distribution of goods is the only challenge.

The liberal politicians make many laws that impinge on capitalism. These policies are aimed at taking a company's profits, its lifeblood, and giving them to others based on political expediency. Taxes are essential for government operation, but a tax that favors resource conservation such as a consumption tax as opposed to one that steals from the productive members of society is the only reasonable tax in an environmentally sensitive capitalistic society.

THE RESURGENCE OF LIBERALISM

I saw the whole stupid system for what it is… the phoniness, the lies,
the corruption, the people working their lives away for nothing.
I do not want to gear my life to the making of money. I do not want to
get ahead. I do not want to occupy a prominent place in his society.
And I decided… that I was against it, that I hated it and
that I would do everything in my power to tear it down.
…and build a better world.
I think a man ought to read and listen to music and philosophize.

—Paul Probius (pseudonym)[47]

---

[47] These quotes are from "Kent State What Happened and Why" by James A. Michener. Fawcett Crest, New York, 1971. They are attributed to Paul Probius, "one of the most powerful radicals enrolled at Kent State" (p. 128). Probius is a pseudonym, as he did not want his real name used. These quotes are from various pages between 128 and 142. They are not necessarily in order but reflect, I believe, the true sentiments of Probius and modern liberals. Traveling SDS (Students for a Democratic Society) activists, such as William Charles "Bill" Ayers (p. 86), visited the Kent State campus several times prior to the riots and were responsible, in part, for the catastrophic deaths. Bernadine Dohrn, the SDS *interorganizational secretary of the national committee*, is noted for her approval of the Manson murders and is quoted as saying "Dig it! First they killed the pigs, then they ate dinner in the same room with them, then they even shoved a fork into a victims' stomach! Wild!" When she visited the Kent State campus, she said "They're certainly going to shoot whites here" p. 85.

The battle of cultures is between the liberal class-based authoritarian cultures and the unique North American capitalist, egalitarian, hard-working, self-reliant, and freedom-based culture. The class-based cultures arose over the last 5,000 years because, as tribes became larger and more numerous, highly structured tribal organizations won out over the other alternatives. The dominant individuals of the tribes became the ruling classes and forced the lower classes to serve their needs and do the everyday work of procuring and preparing food, clothing, and shelter. The ruling classes controlled the productive and military resources of the tribe. In class-based cultures, the upper classes look down upon physical labor. The upper classes do not do physical work; it is beneath them. Their contribution to society is, as Probius desires, ruling, listening to music, and philosophizing.

In response to a domineering ruling class, the social compact movement evolved in Northern Europe and promoted the concept that hard work is a contribution to society and is worthy in and of itself. These ideas greatly influenced the early American freedom-based cultures to where they became instinctual in American tribalism. In America, the self-made man is deemed more worthy and competent than a person who was born to an elitist upper class. American tribalism rejects the liberal European concept of a society based on hereditary ruling classes running all-powerful governments.

The free American tribal culture evolved over the first 200 years of our country but since early in the nineteen hundreds, the ruling classes have tried to reestablish themselves and reintroduce the old liberal authoritarian governmental policies. The progression of liberalism in America has been slow but steady. Liberal radicals use national emergencies to enhance their power. For example, during the Great Depression, Franklin D. Roosevelt instituted the Social Security Act which is the largest governmental transfer of wealth in the world comprising over 20 percent of the national budget. FDR's superior ruling class mentality is demonstrated by his actions. He violated the spirit of the Constitution's three independent branches of government by proposing to pack the Supreme Court with his appointees so that it would not declare portions of his New Deal program unconstitutional. He dishonored the long-standing tradition of a two-term limitation on the presidency. The two-term tradition was an explicit rejection of the establishment of a ruling class by President Washington. Even today, certain *upper-class* families, such as the Roosevelts, the Kennedys, the Clintons, and the Bushes, try to dominate local and national government based on their hereditary credentials.

The demonstrations and riots staged in the Vietnam War era were ostensibly antiwar, but they were designed to destroy the pre-seventies' successful capitalistic, dynamic small tribe American culture and reestablish a class-structured mega-tribe world society. At the time of the Vietnam demonstrations, the American economic class structure was more or less egalitarian—the majority of the population was of the middle class. However, as history has shown, the ruling classes are always striving to come out on top and extend their power. By Probius's own words, he is a ruling class liberal. He does not want to work. He wants to philosophize. He wants to do his own thing as long as it is not work. Liberals want a worldwide tribal society where there is no personal responsibility and no one has to do anything they don't want to. Probius and his liberal companions were not only willing to but intended to destroy American society to obtain his lazy, selfish goals. Kent State was a test ground for violent liberal activism in America. The Kent State tragedy, in the eyes of liberal activists, was not that five innocent students were killed but that the public reaction was against the instigators of the violence, not the establishment. Bill Ayers (a co-founder of Students for a Democratic Society) and Bernardine Dohrn (a leader in the Weather Underground) and other liberals learned that they could not change American culture violently and abruptly. They learned that liberal ideals must be instilled in the form of instincts over multiple generations.

Liberals have attacked the American culture on multiple fronts, but three are most obvious. First, they have taken over the educational system so that they can indoctrinate children with their liberal mega-tribe world point of view. They use the public school system to condition the population to have instinctual liberal reactions to fearful crises when the appropriate *emotional* situations such as *gun violence* are invoked. Environmental items are favorite Pavlovian bells. For example, any mention of *polar bears* is designed to trigger an instinctual attitude in favor of governmental regulation of carbon dioxide emission to *prevent* the *threat* of global warming.

The takeover of the education system is most pronounced at the university level. The self-proclaimed elitist educational institutions, such as Harvard, Yale and Princeton, that were originally established to promote the social compact beliefs of religious freedom, hard work, self-reliance, and equality of citizenry are now dedicated to educating apparatchiks for the ruling class-based US bureaucracy. In order to achieve this goal, these institutions have promoted the concept that the only form of intelligence is memorization. That is, they prize the ability to read and memorize liberal propaganda and then spit back the liberal point of view on command. They claim to but in fact do not embrace original thought. Even the *scientific* and engineering communities prize conformity. For example, Harvard's President Lawrence Summers was forced to resign because he stated a position on a scientific theory not accepted by the liberal faculty. The debate on global warming is due in part to the refusal of the liberal power structure to print and disseminate ideas opposing their point of view. They are cognizant of the fact that those that shout the loudest and longest often get their way. Unfortunately, the positions of those that shout the loudest and longest are often wrong.

The imperialistic class-based societies of Europe often exercised control by prohibiting educating the conquered cultures and lower classes. This approach still exists in a modified form today in Europe and America where the masses are restricted to the *lesser* institutions. These *lesser* universities and schools have been co-opted to educate the *lower* classes so that they can support both the *ruling* classes, the overbearing governmental infrastructure, and the lower classes[48] whose votes are bought by governmental wealth redistribution.

---

[48] Please be aware that *lesser* and *lower* are only used in the manner that class-based liberals would use them. That is, these terms refer to liberal perceived class status only, not quality or integrity.

Second, liberals have attacked the maintenance and procreation of small tribes. A feeling of belonging, worthiness, and a need to contribute to the tribe are inherent small tribal instincts essential for tribal cohesiveness and survival. Many religious congregation in America, in addition to faith, rely on the intimacy of the small group atmosphere to promote a sense of security, belonging, well-being, and solidarity. In the early years of American culture, religious and charitable organizations provided the direction and means for contributing to the small tribal society. The altruistic cultural instincts were satisfied by personal sacrifice for the good of the tribe. These instincts are perhaps most noticeable in the religious and medical area. As a case in point, consider the Good Samaritan hospitals, the Sisters of Mercy, and other charitable Jewish and Islamic hospitals. Individuals involved in such organizations often sacrificed personal comfort and reward for the satisfaction of helping their fellow man. They were rewarded by the primitive but powerful sense of small tribal belonging and social interconnectedness. The liberal movement has systematically reduced the importance of these sacrifices by taking them over as a duty of the government.

Liberals feel that they are meeting their obligation to society by forcing others through government edict and taxation to do so. When the liberal ruling class directs the government to perform these duties, the social interconnectedness of the action dies. An individual who may achieve some feeling of contributing to the tribe receives no benefit because the *contribution* is forced through taxation. The government worker received no personal satisfaction or emotional benefit because they are being paid for just doing a job. Thus, the personal cohesiveness of the small tribe is eliminated by an uncaring, impersonal government. This is an intentional attempt to destroy the altruistic cultural instincts of the small tribe, in general, and religion-based organizations, in particular, as they are the prominent instantiations of philanthropic tribal organizations.

Third is the liberal media. By dominating the educational system, the liberals have been able to dominate the staffing of news media with reporters that want to *make a difference in the world,* not report the news. To that end, news reporters and liberal commentators who cannot mount an argument to an opposing position resort to shouting, bringing up red herrings,[49] and calling names. All these mechanism are taught as legitimate *debating* techniques at liberal schools. When all else fails, they propose closing down opposing speech in violation of the First Amendment. Recently, liberals have favored a *fairness doctrine* which would require all public broadcasts to present equal time to all points of view until they realized that most public broadcasts are steeply biased in favor of liberal points of view. Now, liberals like columnist Paul Krugman are calling for censorship of conservative ideas.[50] Liberal Senator John Kerry wants to prevent opposition outright. He said recently that the media "has got to begin to not give equal time or equal balance" to opposing ideas.[51]

Liberalism, *progressivism*, or socialism by any name is not a new, better form of society. It is a movement to return to the class-based societies of Europe with the *intelligent* ruling class on top and the lower classes on the bottom so that they can be kept ignorant of the true nature of the situations. The liberals are able to control the electorate majority by making the productive minority of individuals pay their *fair share*, while exempting the lower majority from paying anything. Over 50 percent of wage earners in the US today do not pay income taxes but instead get a *refund* payment in exchange for their vote to keep the liberal class in power. Liberals are able to install this mega-tribal class-based society on us because of their powerful propaganda machine and our primitive tribal instincts for security, to *classify* people, and to trust our leaders.

Liberals, like socialists, communists, and Nazis,[52] state that they are moving toward a new, more just society for the *common* man.

---

[49] "*Red herring* is an idiomatic expression referring to the rhetorical or literary tactic of diverting attention away from an item of significance." *The American Heritage Dictionary of the English Language*, Fourth Edition. Revised February 04, 2009.

[50] July 26, 2011.

[51] The "Morning Joe" show August 5, 2011.

[52] Liberals claim that Nazism is right-wing, but it is a form of socialism. Nazism is a society in which the industries are controlled to support the goals of government and *for the benefit of the people*. Liberals are in favor of Nazi principles. For example, GM was saved by the government for the benefit of the unions and,

But, in fact, the free American capitalist society of the nineteenth and twentieth centuries that they are trying to replace is the most just, effective, and productive society yet devised by man. This free capitalist society is a sophisticated, advanced culture based on small tribal instincts which evolved out of the rejection of the mega-class-based societies of Europe. In the class-based societies, even today, one's future and well-being, to a large extent, is based on one's birth and *family connections*, not ability or contribution to society. In the free American capitalist society, everyone is born free of the stigma of a *lower class* or *backward* birth and upbringing. An individual's future is based on one's hard work and ability to create wealth. The result is more wealth for society as a whole. Free market capitalism, not class-based big government socialism, is the reason that hundreds of thousands want to join our society. Immigrants come to the US to work hard and live in freedom, not to bathe in the *liberal luxuries* of a nanny state. Unfortunately, now that the educational system has been taken over by liberals and the media tamed, the violent side of liberalism is beginning to be unleashed.

American liberalism is a de-evolution of society from a free capitalistic society to a classist, racist society controlled by liberals for the benefit of the liberal leadership. An Article V Constitution Convention is the only way to circumvent the liberal mentality instilled by the media, educators, and politicians.

---

in return, the company must produce impractical, uneconomic electric cars for the betterment of society at government edict, and the union must support the liberal government with contributions and votes.

Liberalism, Socialism, and Communism

All animals are equal, but some animals are more equal than others.
—George Orwell, *Animal Farm*

The underlying goal of the liberal, progressive, socialist, and communist movements is to establish a ruling class to govern mega-tribes using the primitive small tribe instincts. Liberalism[53] espouses many of the primitive tribal instincts and principles outlined in "It takes a village."[54] The well-being of the entire village is foremost and a joint effort. The ultimate goal of these philosophies is the establishment of a global tribe with a global liberal nobility to rule over the distribution of the world's limited resources[55] to the lower classes. The imposition of these ideas on mega-tribe nations and a one-world tribe requires a strong class-based hierarchy dominated by a powerful ruling class and mega-government to implement their edicts.

To achieve control, liberals rely on the powerful, primitive, lazy tribal instincts that evolved in the time of limited resources and a hostile world environment. Liberals feel that they are filling the necessary leadership roles that evolved in these ancient times. Liberal

---

[53] Liberalism is used as a general term for liberal, progressive, socialistic, and communistic ideals.

[54] Hillary Rodham Clinton. *It Takes a Village: And Other Lessons Children Teach Us*. Simon and Schuster. New York, 1996.

[55] Recent statements by liberals confirm that they even consider your children a resource that they should control.

leaders feel they are smarter than the rest of the population and that they do not need to take heed of tribal intelligence and that the individuals in the lower classes are incapable of making intelligent decisions. Thus, it is their duty to make the tough decisions for the lower classes. The *upper classes* are to be supported by the lower classes in exchange for the security of a minimal subsistence in the form of a *living* wage. The working classes are held in virtual slavery where they are *given* or allowed to earn only enough to survive at the *poverty* level. The excess income earned by those above the poverty level is taxed away by the government for redistribution to the *less fortunate*. By taxing away excess cash, the liberal government prevents families from saving for emergencies and/or retirement, in effect perpetuating the reliance on government transfer payments for sickness and old age, and at the same time buying the votes of the *lower* classes.

Unfortunately, there is no control on a ruling class in a mega-tribe. The primitive, selfish instincts of selfishness and greed are not controlled by the small tribe altruistic instincts in a mega-tribe because the relationships are impersonal. Thus, there is no control on stealing or corruption. Taking money or property from one class and giving it to another in return for their support is the height of class-based corruption. It is claimed that the class from which the property was taken must contribute their *fair share* to society, but the class to which the property is given need not contribute anything except their votes and children. But the forced taking of tax money is thievery. The removal of children from parental control because they belong to the state is tantamount to slavery. It makes no difference if the taking is by a gun, by social pressure, or by taxes in a corrupted political class-based system.

The loss of freedom required to institute a one-world mega-tribe government is of no consequence to the ruling class as they are above their own edicts. However, the lower classes suffer greatly. Currently, one's inherited citizenry can be changed via personal freedom. That is, if a citizen of a state or country determines that an alternative state or country has a better government, he can, perhaps with some difficulty, change his citizenship. However, with a one-world government, changing *nationality* would be impossible. The ruling class would have unlimited power and the citizens would be in a virtual state of slavery. They may be allowed to change their *nationality*, but they would not be allowed to change their class status. The ruling class would tax the productive classes to any extent necessary to extend benefits to their client classes to maintain their power base. In this liberal feudal system, all of the small tribal altruistic instincts are lost and the result is a battle between classes.

Liberal leaders of the ruling class justify their actions because they believe that only by a powerful ruling class can *equality and justice* be brought to everyone in a one-world tribe. But the tribal instincts that liberal leaders believe in and want to use to control the masses evolved in primitive tribal environments. The more advanced American culture tribalism instincts of freedom, hard work, and responsibility are based on the social compact theories of the seventeenth century and are in direct conflict with the liberals' lazy instincts. As a result, the liberals are now trying to reestablish the primitive selfish instincts in American society via propaganda and indoctrination. They have *dumbed* down the public schools and restrict access to the best *elite* schools to the privileged and client classes. As a case in point, President Obama sent his children to a prestigious private school, but he has closed down the very successful charter school system in Washington D.C., in effect, restricting the *lower* classes to the inferior public schools. More generally, the self-proclaimed *elite* Ivy League schools are very selective of the rich and well-connected students[56] and are dedicated to indoctrinating then with liberal, socialistic ideals so that they will make good ruling class citizens.

The democratic socialistic societies of Europe have evolved from the mega-tribe class structure feudal period. The class structure of the mega-tribes still persists, although somewhat reduced, in these cultures in spite of the economic improvement of the lower classes.

---

[56] Some will argue that these schools go out of their way to supply scholarships to the poor and needy. Frequently, potential students must submit essays as part of the admission process. The essays are just one way the institutions are able to select liberally-inclined students from the lower classes that are likely to support the liberal class-based system.

In a class- based mega-tribe structure, it is difficult to move from a lower class to a higher class. Consequently, there is no incentive to contribute to society and, as a result, there is no social restraining force on the selfish and lazy instincts. There is no force to be responsible for oneself. In socialistic societies, the welfare of the lower class individual is dependent on the welfare of the tribe, generally, and the individual classes in particular. The only distinction in prosperity is based on class division. There is no reward for working hard. The class structure of big liberal governments stifles the competitive, selfish instinct to advance to a higher social class since class status is based on birth, not one's actual contribution to society.

The traditional definition of egalitarian given in the 1989 edition of Webster's Encyclopedic Unabridged Dictionary is *belief in the equality of all men*. This traditional definition has recently been expanded somewhat by liberals to be more politically correct. The Web definitions range from 1) "belief that all people are, in principle, equal and should enjoy equal social, political, and economic rights and opportunities;"[57] 2) "belief in the equality of all people, especially in political, economic, or social life;"[58] and 3) "a social philosophy advocating the removal of inequalities among people."[59] The clear original meaning is meant to eliminate the class distinctions and inequalities in the European cultures. But physical inequalities, such as height, weight, and eyesight, like intelligence, have normal distributions, with some people very gifted, others not so. Other inequalities, such as the location of one's birth or the selection of one's parents, are *accidental*. Liberalism cannot remove these inequalities by changing the definitions of words. Even a worldwide government cannot change these inequalities and can only achieve equality by lowering standards for all. The result is that the least gifted are supported with a welfare *safety net* by the government to satisfy their basic needs. But, at the same time, excess governmental regulation and taxation prevents the gifted from contributing to the wealth of

---

[57] http://encarta.msn.com/dictionary_1861607627/egalitarian.html

[58] http://dictionary.reference.com/browse/egalitarian

[59] http://www.merriam-webster.com/dictionary/egalitarianism

society to their full extent. The ultimate outcome is that the *fortunate* few are penalized to create *equal* but inferior outcomes for all (except for the ruling class which is above all limitations).

The results of liberal *egalitarian* policies are inferior psychologically, as well as economically. Science has shown that helping others produces hormones in the brain that promotes well-being, the state of being happy, healthy, or prosperous, and prolongs life. Thus, liberals that play on the insecure instincts by giving subsistent living conditions in exchange for votes are not promoting the welfare of their clients but actually decreasing it. There is a feeling of satisfaction that comes from fulfilling your own needs and performing a job well. This is what the social compact proponents realized when they formulated the concept that hard work is a reward in and of itself. The positive effect of contributing to society was illustrated by welfare reform in the late 1990s. The effect was so positive that the Obama administration had to cancel the reform to prevent its effectiveness from becoming well-known. It is a sad oxymoron that liberal state *welfare* is detrimental to well-being.

The liberal concept of the *security* in a mega-tribe has several flaws. First, there is no mechanism to assure that everyone contributes to the tribal welfare and adheres to mega-government rules and laws. There is no mechanism to reward individuals for their efforts. As a result, many liberals do not have any pride in themselves or their country because they feel they are a failure and only obtained what they need through the beneficence of the mega-government. They have no confidence that they can achieve a living on their own (without governmental help). Many liberals hide this insecurity by claiming they are the best and smartest but, ultimately, there is no motivation. There is no esprit de corps. There is no common spirit of comradeship, enthusiasm, or devotion to a cause among the members of a group.

Since the liberal class-based structure requires the suppression of individual freedom and initiative, it creates inter-class conflicts. In addition, liberalism magnifies, not reduces, the negative, lazy, selfish tribal instincts at all class levels. As a result, the lower classes become demanding of more resources at the expense of the other classes and the ruling class, by fulfilling these *needs*, feels it is justified in obtaining expensive perks for itself by any means, legal or illegal. The sad truth is that the outdated liberal idea of a class-based utopia of happy, content citizens has been tried many times with tribes of all sizes, failing every time it has been tried. In their zeal to achieve this happy state, liberal leaders have, in the past and will in the future, lie to, steal from, intimidate, and kill those that stand in their way.

Liberal class-structured societies depend on inter-class conflict, and catastrophe has always been the outcome. In order to avoid the penalties of class-structured societies, the constitution must prohibit any law that favors one class over another, whether the class division is based on race, economic status, social status, health, or any other criteria.

POLITICAL PERSUASION

Effective utilization of your vote requires intelligence. Intelligence is defined as the capacity to make choices based on weighing possible consequences. It includes the ability to evaluate the political message and think and reason new responses to new arguments and events in addition to the learned instinctual responses to past arguments. These capabilities are essential when deciding whether to vote for one politician over another.

Politicians use political *persuasion* to convince you to vote for them. The skill of political persuasion is to phrase your legislative goals to appeal to the instincts of your constituents so they will vote for you without thinking. It is a form of brainwashing. Political brainwashing is a process in which a group, such as a political party and/or news media, systematically uses methods such as lies, falsehoods, and misinformation[60] to persuade voters to conform to their wishes, often to the detriment of the voters being manipulated. The term refers to any tactic which subverts an individual's sense of control over their own thinking, behavior, emotions, or decision-making. By repeating the same slur, pejorative, *fact,* or slogan and ignoring facts over and over, these groups can induce instinctual voting patterns.

To understand the use of brainwashing on the masses consider the intentional rebranding of moral, ethical traditions to justify political goals—for example, *a woman's right to choose.* Traditionally, since the beginning of time, it has been a crime against the tribe

---

[60] Ignoring or not reporting pertinent facts and news is just as dishonest as outright lies.

and society for one member of a tribe to kill another member of the tribe. The success and well-being of a tribe depends on expanding its human resources and replacing old life with new. All traditional tribal stories, taboos, and customs call for the mother to sacrifice her well-being, even her life for her offspring. This traditional tribal morality was changed by liberal politicians by substituting the term *a woman's right to choose* for abortion and by redefining fetal life.

According to the dictionary, "abortion is the expulsion of the human fetus within the first twelve weeks of pregnancy, before it is viable."[61] This definition is somewhat confusing since a developing offspring is medically referred to as an embryo up to eight weeks after conception and a fetus only thereafter. The distinction being that in a fetus, the heart, hands, feet, brain, and other organs are distinguishable. In any case, by substituting the term *a woman's right to choose* for abortion, today, a woman has the *right* to kill her child up to the point of it obtaining its first breath and even afterward, according to President Obama. By historical definition, aborting a viable fetus is murder—a crime against the tribe and society. This crime is rationalized by liberals by claiming that a fetus is a part of a woman's body, just as a freckle or wart. They have *dumbed* down American education so that they can get away with this claim. Every educated person knows a fetus is a separate living life—separated from the mother by the placenta. A fetus has its own heart; its own brain, its own life, its own soul. Liberals have perverted the noble maternal instincts of motherhood for the political support of selfish, lazy, insecure women.

The intentional deception of liberal political discussion is further illustrated by the rules of argument taught in the debating classes in Ivy League schools and elsewhere. First and foremost, the relevancy and accuracy of a *fact* is unimportant, it is the number of points and the emotional and instinctual responses that they engender that counts. Studies have shown that those that shout the loudest and longest usually win—but they are usually wrong.

---

[61] Webster's Unabridged Dictionary of the English Language. Portland House. New York, 1989.

Many politicians feel they must outshout their opponents because they do not understand the counterarguments and so cannot defend their own position with rational arguments, only noise. As a result, they fill their shouting with as many *facts* as possible, whether accurate or not. When they finally realize that the facts are not on their side, they are too committed to admit they are wrong and shout even louder. Consider former vice president Al Gore and the global warming *debate* as an example.

Voters have a responsibility to their fellow tribal members to make intelligent decisions. They can only do so if they have honest and accurate information. Honest politicians need to confront self-serving politicians with the true facts and call them out for their lies, irrelevant facts, and misinformation. They need to understand that politics is a tribal fight to the death, not an enlightened, intellectual debate. Which is worse, the abortionist or the politician who claims to be against abortion but will not fight to stop it? It is sad that some politicians will buy the vote of mothers who want to kill their child at the expense of the life of the unborn child to which the constitution guarantees *life, liberty, and the pursuit of happiness.*

Since it is very difficult to prove that a politician is lying or misleading his constituents, a method is needed to assure that politicians are sincere in their legislative duties. One possibility is a constitutional provision that prevents elected officials from exempting themselves from the laws they pass.

CONSERVATISM

Conservatism can be summarized as the belief that individual happiness can most effectively be achieved by continuing the evolution of the American social compact culture via the establishment of a plethora of dynamic, small tribal organizations based on the primitive, selfish, and altruistic instincts, freedom, and capitalism. Just as the primitive, selfish instincts were sublimated by the altruistic instincts to produce an effective tribal organization that evolved over tens of thousands of years, modern free democratic societies' laws, attitudes, and dynamic tribalism have controlled the primitive capitalistic instincts for maximizing profits at any expense. In America, the *evils* of capitalism can be controlled by a free, educated, dynamic tribal society and a small government.

The Declaration of Independence says the *pursuit* of happiness, not the *guarantee* or *delivery* of happiness. When an individual is unhappy with his church, club, or social organization, he can quit and join another. When he is unhappy in his job, he can pursue happiness by quitting and joining another company, by starting a new company, by changing careers, by getting more education, and obtaining employment at a high level, etc. There are many paths to pursue happiness. It is the task of the government to assure that the *paths* are available and that everyone is free to pursue them, not to deliver happiness. The conservative interpretation of egalitarian could be summarized as a belief in the equal opportunity of all people to pursue happiness.

Conservatives believe that government cannot deliver happiness because happiness is different for every individual. A *one size fits all* definition of happiness is not possible. This is why the Declaration of Independence states *pursuit*. The Declaration also states that *liberty* or freedom is an *unalienable right*. The freedom to quit one tribal association (a company, religion, club, or government) and join another tribe (company, religion, club, or government) in pursuit of happiness is *unalienable*. It is a right that cannot be given or taken away. Every individual must decide for himself what determines his happiness. It is his responsibility to exercise his freedom to pursue that happiness.

In a free, conservative, egalitarian, capitalistic society, it is the responsibility of a small government to be an effective force against any unfairness of the economic system that the individual cannot address. In contrast, in a liberal democrat, socialist, communist, or Nazi society, the economic machine is a part of the government so there can be no effective system of checks and balances. Liberal leaders reject the traditional American path to pursue happiness. They reject teaching a universal English language, accepting competence in any language as equivalent. Competence in a common universal language is critical for social acceptance and success. They reject the Protestant ethic of needing to work for a living by providing long-term poverty assistance programs. They reject the concept of small governance as established by the Mayflower Compact. And they reject the capitalistic concept of resource creation, relying solely on resource redistribution. Consequently, liberal leaders condemn their followers and any country they rule to a second-class status.

As an example of the failure of liberal approach, consider that in the traditional American culture, parents and responsible adults realize that many gifts are not appreciated by the receiver to the same degree as the giver. Thus, it is not uncommon to require teenagers to get a job to pay for the car, or at least for the insurance, so that they realize the value of a dollar. Liberals do not understand this aspect of human nature. They *gave* houses to anyone that wanted one by reducing the down payment to zero. The *buyer* did not have to work to obtain a down payment and therefore had no sweat equity, and since the funding was provided by the government, there was no social pressure to make a *responsible* decision. The consequence of this action was, of course, a disaster and the primary reason for the great recession. Ultimately, few benefited other than the powerfully connected and the politicians whose vote was bought by sweetheart deals. But many were harmed, especially those who bought housing they could not afford and became underwater when the bubble burst.

Fixing congresspersons' income to their constituents' median income for the duration of their tenure plus five years post tenure would ensure that they voted for laws that were beneficial to their constituents and prevent them from personally benefiting from intentional or unintentional aspects of the laws they pass.

POLITICS

How do politicians get away with lies and propaganda? "The roots of deceit lie deep in our biological past. Deceptive creatures have an edge... in the relentless struggle to survive and reproduce. Lies and deception helped our species to succeed... So natural selection made them *part of our nature*."[62] In today's politics, the political leaders often use lies and our instincts to control the rest of the tribe. Political lies are designed to create emotion, but it is instincts, not emotions, that cause us to act. As was explained in **Human Intelligence**, instinct is a natural and unreasoning prompting to action. Emotion is a strong feeling—for example, fear, anger, disgust, grief, joy, or surprise. Instinct can include emotional responses, but instinct does not require strong feeling, only *unreasoning* prompting to action. No thinking is involved in instinctual responses to fear, whether emotional or not.

"Our brains seem to have been designed to allow the fear system to take control in threatening situations and *prevent* our conscious awareness from reigning."[63] The primitive amygdala part of our brain records indelible memories of negative emotions and traumatic situations, such as fear, so that the next time a similar situation occurs we can react instinctively, immediately without thinking. "Like all emotions, the fear circuitry steers the organism toward desirable states—away from predators or other threats—without knowing

---

[62] Attributed to Dr. Smith. University of New England. Biddeford, Maine. "In Explaining How We Got This Way, Beware Of the Just-So Story." Sharon Begley. *The Wall Street Journal*, 2004.

[63] "Negative Emotions." *Discover*. March 2003, pp. 38–39.

that much in advance about the world that the organism will actually inhabit. [Emotions] propel us in directions that our rational minds don't always understand."[64]

Over time, the primitive amygdala region of the brain has been trained via evolution to associate the fear memory with defensive responses. When we see a bear, we run. When we see a snake, we freeze. But the amygdala can be retrained to associative fears with other instinctual responses. This primitive part of the brain is present in fruit flies, marine snails, and lizards. These animals, as was well as humans, can be trained to display a specific behavior in response to a stimulus. Over eons, pre-tribal evolution trained the primitive human fear system about physical threats, such as snakes and lions. Current liberal tribal evolution is training the human fear system about reactions to new *social tribal* fears such as isolation (in old age), starvation (of our children), and abandonment (of health care).

The amygdala is the primitive, non-reasoning, part of the brain that many politicians use to achieve political power. Many politicians and their cohorts want to retrain the amygdala to instinctively respond negatively against their political rivals when the social tribal fear memories are triggered. Politicians, supporting political organizations, and propagandists lie to create negative, fearful images to condition their constituents—like Pavlov conditioned his dogs—not to vote for them but to vote against their rivals without thinking. This explains the success of *negative campaigning*. Some politicians use people's innate fear of starvation, isolation, abandonment in old age, etc. to condition voters to be afraid of rivals by repeatedly associating them with these negative images. Some politicians use their constituents' selfish, lazy instincts to obtain votes by implying that they do not need to work for their basic needs, it is their right to the world's limited resources and the government will see that they get their share. They, like Probius, do not see work as having any intrinsic value as espoused in the social compact and Protestant ethic, but *people are working their lives away for nothing*. The people conditioned

---

[64] "Negative Emotions." *Discover*. March 2003, p. 39.

by these methods are the so-called *mind-numbed masses* so revered by the liberals.

Some biologists believe that conditioned responses can be passed from generation to generation. Thus, political organizations are using them to change the American culture. One example of such a situation is multiculturalism. A basic tenet of the American culture up until the 1970s and 1980s was that America was a melting pot with one culture. At that time, schools taught one standard American English language to unify the American tribe. The liberals realized that an America unified by a common culture and language was too powerful to overcome. So, like in the story of the Tower of Babel, they decided to break up this unity by introducing different cultures and languages. They realized that tribes are united by a common language and that language is one of the most important distinguishing characteristics between rival warring tribes. So they claimed that other cultural practices and languages spoken by immigrants were just as good as the American culture and English.[65] They forced schools to teach classes in the immigrants' native language instead of requiring the students to learn English as has had been the custom for over hundreds of years. As a result, today, the American public has been conditioned to accept multiculturalism without question. The American psyche has been conditioned to reject anyone who points out the disservice done to immigrants, minorities, and their descendants that cannot speak American English well.[66] The sole purpose of this brainwashing is to create multiple weak classes which speak substandard English so that they can be pitted against each other via class warfare for political advantage.

The individual altruistic instinct upon which the humanitarian nature of liberalism depends actually works against the tribe as a whole. Hobbes claimed that people will trade their instinct for freedom for the satisfaction of the primitive instincts for safety, food, and

---

[65] The issue was never one of the *quality* of a language, but only the necessity of merging the immigrants into the American culture for the benefit of all.

[66] "Pygmalion" by George Bernard Shaw illustrates the effect of *proper* grammar and English in society.

essential resources.[67] That is, people's primitive instincts for laziness and selfishness can override their instinct for freedom. The ruling class uses this propensity to establish their position and control over the *lower* classes in large mega-tribes. This trade-off weakens the society as a whole as there is little or no tribal altruism. That is, if one's needs are satisfied by the mega-tribe, there is no incentive to create or distribute new resources. The government will take the resources you need from others, diminishing the overall wealth of the tribe.

In order to overcome the public's perception of political deceit, politicians must be held accountable for their actions. One way to achieve this is to amend the Constitution so that politicians are rewarded for the laws they pass in the same manner and degree as their constituents.

---

[67] John Briggs. "Social Compact Theory." www.ehow.com.

Restoring Small Tribal Principles

Conservatives want to restore the American tribal society that was established on this continent. The American tribal society replaced the old elitist ruling class-based societies that evolved over the last 5,000 years with a strong dynamic American tribal system. Among these enhancements were the right for (small) groups of people to create social compacts (governments), to own personal property that the tribe cannot take away, the freedom to pursue happiness by employing their personal property for financial gains, the rejection of any static/inherited class-based system, and the belief that any type of work or physical labor is worthy and is a valuable contribution to society. Conservatives feel that an important component of happiness is a sense of pride, well-being, and accomplishment achieved by work itself and the possession of resources procured by work.

Like Hobbes, conservatives feel that happiness is most easily achieved in small democratic tribal organizations with individual freedom. Like Hobbes, conservatives do not accept evil selfish people. But unlike Hobbes who was exposed only to European classist capitalism and felt that the tribal communities were dedicated to trade because of limited resources, American conservatives feel that the inter-tribal competition of free market capitalism creates a surplus of resources that results in trade and, ultimately, the maximal improvement in the overall wealth of all the tribes.

The federal government is the only political structure in America which has no competition. If the federal government imposes an oppressive law or tax in the name of *fairness*, the people affected do not have a constitutional right to move to another country. There is no recourse other than to fight by an appeal to another branch of the same oppressive government. Ultimately, as the federal government becomes more and more oppressive, the fight will become violent. In order to prevent this, the constitution severely restricted the power of the federal government. But over the last one hundred years, these restrictions have been ignored and overruled. Conservatives believe that the best way to advance Hobbs's small tribe social compact ideas in the modern world is to restore the restrictions on the federal government and to control the excesses of capitalism and government by a well-educated egalitarian population.

Conservatives realize that tribal societies of any size require *laws and taboos*, but these controls should be made at as low a governmental level as possible and they should be minimal. They feel that *small* social contracts like the Mayflower Compact are much more effective and humane than the impersonal ruling class mega-government favored by liberals. They feel that the tribal altruistic instinct is much more effective present in small tribes for delivering social services. So, as many social services as possible, such as health services, feeding the hungry, patrolling the neighborhoods, education, should be done at the local level by charities or, if necessary, by the city or county governments. Achieving these goals at the local personal level imparts a feeling of belonging that big governmental bureaucracy cannot deliver. Hobbes realized that people will trade their freedom for the impersonal delivery of essential needs, such as safety and food. Conservatives feel that trading freedom for security from a mega-tribal government is demeaning and results in a loss of self-esteem and an overall reduction in tribal well-being and happiness. Conservatives feel that only those services which cannot be handled locally by a small tribal government such as inter-city road design and construction, disaster response, and state-wide utilities such as water for irrigation should be passed to the state government. Finally, the national government should only perform those duties that cannot be done by the states, such as interstate commerce and common defense.

The original intention of the Founding Fathers was a limited national government. They did not intend for the Supremacy Clause (Article VI) to enable the national government to impose ever burdensome laws on the various states. One issue that an Article V Convention could address is a strengthening of state rights by allowing states to opt out of any federal program and have the money collected from the state for the program to be returned directly to the state.

CONCLUSION

A capitalistic culture, as espoused by today's conservative movement, is dependent on maximal freedom to allow individuals to achieve their goals. A socialistic culture, as espoused by today's liberal movement, suppresses individual freedoms so that society can provide the wants, not the needs, of the most individuals at the expense of the productive individuals. Understanding how these social organizations relate to one another is essential for an intelligent discussion of which culture is most appropriate for us and our children. The table in Appendix B juxtaposes the differences illustrating why American capitalism is superior to liberalism.

Even today, Homo sapiens are still controlled by two sets of emotions and instincts. The selfish instincts which evolved in a hostile environment are greed, gluttony, hoarding, and laziness. These instincts evolved at a time when food and other needs were thought to be grudgingly provided by nature. The mentality was to satisfy only the immediate needs resulting in the perception of limited resources. This perception is the reason for the conflict within tribes and warfare between tribes. The altruistic instincts of sharing, compassion, empathy, and helping the sick and elderly evolved with the beginning of tribalism and having a coterie of friends. The secure environment that the altruistic instincts create relays a feeling of hope and confidence in the future. The altruistic instincts are the reasons for intratribal cooperation. Both sets of instincts evolved over the generations pitting one tribal culture against another.

Because of limited resources due to a lack of technology in earlier times, competition with other tribes was intense. As a result, inter-tribal warfare became the most dominant of all the tribal instincts. It is the principle of survival of the fittest which brought human society to where it is today. The result of the current conflict between the liberal class-based culture and the conservative capitalistic culture will determine our future as a species. But the nature of that culture may not be the one anticipated or desired by the most people. The class-based liberal socialist culture intends to assure maximum benefits to the ruling class and minimal, but secure[68] benefits to their lower client classes. The conservative free capitalist-based culture will provide maximal rewards for all but requires everyone to work to the best of their ability and contribute to the general welfare.

Karl Marx felt that society evolved from feudalism to capitalism to socialism. He realized that private property was central to capitalism and felt it was the reason for two classes of people—the bourgeoisie (owners) and the proletariat (the workers). In essence, the feudal ruling class evolved into the bourgeoisie and then into the *enlightened* liberal ruling class, while the feudal serfs evolved into the proletariat and then into the dependent client classes. Marx lived in a class-based culture. He did not feel that individuals could move from one class to another. The argument here is that social evolution is not a straight line but branches significantly when the primitive tribal instinct of freedom is introduced to capitalism. Both feudalism and socialism suppress egalitarianism and freedom so that a powerful ruling class can distribute societal wealth to their client classes to maintain their power. But American culture is based on free men in an egalitarian society free of class distinctions where private property allows anyone regardless of the status of their birth to elevate themselves to any level in society that they desire. American cultural capitalism is an evolutionary branch off of the mainline ruling class continuum. Modern liberals are trying to force the American capitalism cultural branch back into the socialist stream by creating a dependency class

---

[68] The benefits will be sold as *secure* but when the lower classes do not get regular increases in their *fair share*, violence will result and the system will break down as has happened many times in history, perhaps the most cited being the decline of the Roman Empire, but is happening more recently in the southern EU countries, such as Greece.

at the expense of personal freedom. They, like Marx, believe that an individual is born into a class and cannot escape it.

Liberal socialism has perverted the primitive instincts to its needs. The instinct that resources were provided by nature was converted into the instinct that resources are provided by a benevolent government. In addition, the inter-tribal warfare instincts were converted into inter-class warfare instincts. The ruling class leaders strive to create class distinctions and barriers so that they can pit one class against another. Liberalism must have class conflict for the survival of the ruling class. To achieve their goal, liberals must sublimate the selfish, amoral tribal instincts to the mega-government so that the ruling class can reap maximal rewards for themselves, while the lower classes enjoy only the minimal *fair* rewards bestowed on them. The ruling class must keep the lower classes in *poverty* (i.e., a state of want and desire[69]) so that they can keep control of the limited resources.

Conservative American capitalism sublimates the selfish, amoral tribal instincts to the plethora of dynamic small tribal entities which flourish in a free society. American Capitalism introduced the idea that resources can be created when needed via hard work. The inter-tribal warfare instinct is civilized in that the conflict is between the dynamic tribes which create the resources. The tribes themselves are created, evolve and die with no loss of human life. When a company, social organization, or local club dies because of competition or the need for it disappears, new entities, companies, and organizations will appear to meet the new needs. Thus conservative American capitalism is the ultimate society, liberal socialist/communist/fascist/ nazist societies are at best penultimate.

Only a minimal government is needed to assure that civilized rules of fair competition are generated and adhered to. If the goal of the American culture is reached—a free, classless society wherein everyone can pursue their individual happiness—there is no need for a ruling class or overbearing government. The reactionary old culture ruling class liberal forces are conducting their last desperate

---

[69] As a case in point, remember that the *poverty* level today includes items such as cell phones and televisions that were considered luxuries a few years ago.

struggle against the revolutionary new American capitalistic conservative cultural forces. The liberal mass media's propagandist support of ruling class liberalism masks their inner weakness—lacking the popular support of the average man and woman.

Liberals and conservatives disagree on many issues, but they have common ground in not believing in the others' politicians. They both believe that the US government and many large city and state governments are corrupt and run by special interest groups. Originally, the US Congress was meant to be a citizen legislative body, but it has evolved into a de facto ruling class. The tendency for leaders to establish themselves as permanent dictators is common throughout history. Indeed, one of the main fears about George Washington was that he would declare himself king after winning the revolutionary war. He did not, and by not doing so set the precedence of peaceful transfer of power from one leader to the next.

Both liberals and conservatives also feel that people should be rewarded for their efforts and successes. Since every member of congress represents a specific set of constituents, the true egalitarian way of rewarding them is to base their compensation on that of their constituents. If a congressman helps pass a law that helps his constituents improve their well-being, his well-being will increase, also. But as a member of the federal government, he is also responsible to the country as a whole. Thus, a portion of his compensation should be based on how well the country as a whole fares. Appendix A contains a draft constitutional amendment to this effect. Such an amendment would alleviate the need for dealing with separate issues, such as a budget ceiling and term limits. If congress will not pass this or a similar amendment via *normal channels*, the states should call an Article V Constitutional Convention to do so.

SECTION 2

American Culture and Politics

THE AMERICAN CULTURE

The unique American culture is a serendipitous blend of social contract concepts, freedom, technology, capitalism, and limited sovereign authority manifested in a plethora of dynamic social and economic small tribal associations and their peaceful interaction for commerce, trade, and the exchange of knowledge.

During the early settlement of North America, it became necessary to establish local governments such as the Mayflower Compact (1620). Social compacts were necessary because it was impractical to rely on laws made on the other side of the Atlantic to address immediate needs in an environment where day-to-day survival was at stake. These social compacts were based in part on the political philosophy of the day as stated by Thomas Hobbes (1588–1679) who claimed that political power is based on the consent of the people. He also promoted the ideas of individual rights, equality, and freedom to do whatever is not explicitly forbidden, and felt that the ultimate human happiness and contentment could be found in small self-governing groups of no more that several hundred people.

The early American colonists were loyal subjects of their kings, but by the time of the American Revolution in 1776, European philosophers such as Jean-Jacques Rousseau (1712–1778) rejected the concepts of the unlimited authority of the ruling class and the divine right of kings. The rejection of these old-world ideas were reinforced in America when George Washington refused to be anointed king and voluntarily limited his presidency to eight years.

The political philosophy of the seventeenth and eighteenth centuries the Industrial Revolution, capitalism and urbanization allowed the development of classical liberalism in the nineteenth century. Classical liberalism should not to be confused with the self-proclaimed liberals and progressives of today. Classical liberalism advocates freedom (individual liberties), limited (i.e., small) government, the rule of law, and economic freedom.

All the components of classical liberalism are fundamental characteristics of the American culture, but the significance of freedom cannot be underestimated. Perhaps the most important sentence in the Declaration of Independence is that which contains the clause: *all men are created equal.* This is the absolute rejection of the limitations imposed by the European class-based society where one's future and potential is determined by his race and who his parents were.

American culture is centered on the freedom of the individual to achieve his dreams. An important component of this realization is education. Initially, the colonies taught their citizens to read so that they could read the Bible, but with a democratic government and the advent of the industrial and technological revolution, the importance of a complete and well-educated public became evident.

In summary, the American culture, which people from around the world take immeasurable risks to take part in, is characterized by:

Freedom—the ability to do anything that is not explicitly forbidden;

Equality—the rejection of racist class-based systems that limit one's ability to achieve their dreams;

Capitalism—the profit motive of self-organized groups competing with one another to provide the public with services and goods; and

Technology—the know-how to convert raw resources into useful products, thus avoiding the need to divide up and redistribute the perceived limited wealth and natural resources.

FREEDOM

*"We hold these truths to be self-evident, that all men are created equal,
that they are endowed by their Creator with certain unalienable rights,
that among these are Life, Liberty and the pursuit of Happiness."*
>   —The Declaration of Independence

The second sentence of the Declaration of Independence must be understood in its entirety and in the environment of the day. Some seventeenth century philosophers felt that happiness was most easily achieved in small democratic tribal organizations with individual freedom. The second clause—*all men are created equal*—of the second sentence is an outright rejection of a class-based society, in general, and a ruling class, specifically. In European society of the time, the ruling class claimed that its lofty status was justified by the divine right of kings—that a monarch was subject to no earthly authority, deriving the right to rule directly from the will of God. The second clause unequivocally states that God gave the right of freedom directly to everyone and that no government had the right to abridge it. It is a restatement of Hobbes's thoughts that political power is based on the consent of the people. It further states that God gave men the right of freedom to pursue happiness—to achieve their dreams for themselves, their family, their children, and their children's future.

The European class-based society, like all class-based societies, determines your fate based on your class at birth. It allocates specific types of jobs for certain classes and asserts that it is the *responsibility* of the *upper* classes to provide for the welfare of the lower classes and at the same time it is demeaning for the upper classes to do lower-class work. The Calvinistic philosophers of the period, however, in rejecting the class-based society proclaimed that all work has merit. The American dream is that freedom allows any responsible person through hard work, regardless of birth status, to pursue and achieve happiness.

Hobbes philosophized that small, free, self-governing groups was the best path to happiness. The sixteenth and seventeenth century philosophers were concerned that in larger, more confrontational societies, people would sacrifice freedom, accepting an unaccountable government for security from the unknown. The modern-day liberals, via the Democrat party, have proved this fear to be real.

Liberals have been trying to reestablish a European class-based society since the 1920s by promising ever more security and a reduction in responsibility, albeit at the cost of the loss of freedom. Americans today must work on average 102 days per year, over twenty weeks, two-fifths or 40 percent of a year to pay for *security* in the form of forced wealth transfers. A large portion of this 40 percent of the economy is spent on supporting the ruling political class.

It has taken almost one hundred years for liberals to indoctrinate the education system to misconstrue the Declaration of Independence's second sentence's meaning to conform to their own designs. Liberals, in direct conflict with the American culture, believe that a class-based society is the only way to bring *happiness* to the lower classes. That is, they feel that the lower classes are incapable of achieving happiness by themselves and that it must be provided by an all-powerful government. They have installed their minions in the education system to brainwash the general population into believing that the Declaration of Independence guarantees equal outcome regardless of effort expended, not equal opportunity for the hardworking to get ahead. Unfortunately, the happiness of the upper and lower classes come at the expense of the freedom and happiness of the middle class which must support the other two. Since many in the middle class do not agree with the philosophy of a class-based society, this is not only a loss of freedom for them but a form of economic slavery.

TRIBALISM

*The basic unit of human evolution is the tribe, not
the individual. Like other social animals, individuals
are born, live and die, but the tribe lives on.*

The special features of the human brain allow the tribe to function as a super being. That is, the sophisticated communication skills that humans have evolved via the FOXP2 gene allow members of a tribe to operate in unison as a single organism, much as the bees in a hive or ants in an anthill. Effective communication and individuals with special talents allow the tribal organism to dynamically morph and reform into different configurations for many different, diverse tasks.

Fighting to obtain wants and needs is standard in the animal world, and is standard for human individuals and tribes. Men fight over women, and tribes fight to control regional resources. The instinct to fight that was instilled over the millennia persists today and is the source of competition in team sports and business. On the negative side, it is the source of crime, political corruption, and warfare between nations.

The traits required for tribal survival for tens of thousands of years in a hostile environment became tribal instincts. In a hostile environment, it is not sufficient to address an issue on an ad hoc basis. Often, the issue must be addressed instinctively without thought. That tribe which was the most successful in evolving the best set of tribal instincts outcompeted the other tribes, dominated, and multiplied.

Human instincts can be roughly organized into two sets which are applied differently on two levels. The selfish instincts of hoarding, greed, gluttony, laziness, etc. evolved for individual survival. The altruistic instincts of sharing, compassion, empathy, needing to contribute to the tribe, helping others, etc. which evolved via group evolution are a critical component of tribalism. Successful tribalism also required the evolution of an instinct to work cooperatively for a common tribal goal such as security and an instinct to follow tribal leaders even into life threatening situations such as big game hunting with only a spear or atlatl or into warfare with competing tribes.

The selfish instincts are the result of hundreds of thousands of years of evolution and still form the basis of our primitive basic human instincts for self-preservation. These pre-tribal pre-human individual instincts such as hoarding food are antisocial, so it was necessary for tribal mechanisms to evolve to control them. For example, peer pressure and the fear of abandonment are powerful mechanisms that compel us instinctively to be kind to others in the tribe and to share. Thus, the individual's instinct to ensure his survival by hoarding food can be overcome by tribal instincts to share food with others for the benefit of the tribe.

Tribal evolution has sublimated the selfish instincts for the well-being of the tribe. Thus, individual hoarding is antisocial, but tribal hoarding of resources such as a prize hunting ground is good. Killing a fellow individual in a tribe is the ultimate in antisocial behavior, but killing an individual of an enemy tribe while defending the hunting ground is perceived as good, even laudatory. The sublimation of the pre-tribal instinct to the tribal level makes the tribe function like a super being. These primitive forces are visible in today's tribal organizations—companies, governments, and social clubs—in the form of cooperation and competition, both friendly and hostile.

Tribalism, as a form of a living being, constantly, although slowly, evolves. In order to accommodate the population explosion enabled by the agricultural and technological breakthroughs of the last 5,000 years, the historical small village tribal structure evolved into a large class-based structure but with the same fundamental restriction of birth placement. Just as in primitive agricultural tribalism where an individual is bound to the village in which he or she is born, in class-based tribalism an individual is bound to the class in which he or she is born regardless of the village to which he or she may migrate.

American tribalism advances the tribal fixed village, fixed class structure with a multitude of dynamic tribal structures which one is free to join and abandon at will. Some of the dynamic tribes are one's job, one's church, one's social groups, and even one's local government. Freedom from the class-based social structure allows any American to advance to any level of society both monetarily and socially to achieve their American dream.

A basic condition for a successful tribal organization is *smallness*. In order for tribal instincts to operate effectively and control individual pre-tribal instincts, everyone in the tribe must know everyone else and be able to judge their needs, desires, and skills. The ability to assess an individual's skills requires *close* contact. Originally, primitive tribes consisted of up to several hundred individuals so that a personal awareness of everyone was possible. Moreover, tribal affiliation was obvious by physical features, clothing, and language. With the development of more advanced means of communication such as writing, more indirect means of judging became possible—for example, by a letter of recommendation or a personal communication by a friend for a friend.

The new communication and transportation technology has allowed the development of a mobile society where individuals are free to move to any location that they feel will allow them to fulfill their dream. But the new location, more than likely, already has tribal customs and restrictions in place to control resources and opportunities. Moving to a new location requires joining the local tribal organizations, such as schools, churches, social clubs, charitable societies, etc. Peaceful integration is achieved by adopting local customs and ways, such as dress and speech, enabling effective communication with the new tribe.

Most tribes are small. However, with the advent of modern communication, organizations of tens of thousands can be effectively run. But there is a limit. It is recognized that organizations, companies, and governments can become bloated and that too many levels of communication between the top and bottom is counterproductive. When this happens, if it is not corrected, the tribal being will eventually die or be killed.

MORALITY AND RELIGION

Religion is omnipresent. Some individuals may be agnostic. Some individuals may be atheist. Some are helpful, charitable, and loving, while others are depraved, selfish, evil, base, and vulgar. But the tribe, as a whole, is religious.

Religion permeates all tribal cultures. Religion sets the rules for morality within and between tribes. Religion provides a sense of security. No matter how hostile the environment, the tribe knows that it will be protected by God. The tribe knows that if it obeys God's laws, God will provide for them. God's laws provide the tribal moral instincts that are passed down from generation to generation. Ultimately, religion molds, shapes, and determines the personality of the tribe.

In class-based societies, religion is the only restraining force on the morality of the ruling class. Kings and queens and the nobility have the power to force their own moral codes on the lower classes. Only God can protect the masses from the ruling class, and only God has the power to force His moral code on the ruling class. Understanding that religion is the only limit on their power, the ultimate goal of the modern liberal ruling class is to destroy God and His control over them. They want to replace Him with government as the protector and provider and the arbiter of moral standards.

Early Americans had freedom of religion. They could obtain comfort and security from the religious tribe of their choice. They could satisfy their earthly needs through hard work and the guidance of their religion. They could satisfy their social charitable instincts by helping their neighbors. If a neighbor became ill, the religious community would feed and care for the rest of the family until no longer needed. During the harvest season, farm families would help one another until all the crops were gathered in from the field, further cementing religious and tribal bonds. If the religious community was threatened by outside forces, the religious community would come together for mutual protection. There was no need for a ruling class to provide charity or security.

In order to establish their power, the ruling class had to devise a scheme to replace religion with government. They knew that they could change the religious culture by slowly assuming the role of the religious community using people's selfish, lazy instincts. Epigenetics[70] would do the rest. The first step was the *invention* of social security. The ruling class was able to transfer the responsibility of caring for one's neighbor to the federal government because of the severe economic need of the nation at the time. By taking the responsibility of caring for the old and destitute off the shoulders of the local population and moving it to a remote, invisible government, it seemed like God had answered their prayers for relief from a moral burden.

The liberal ruling class elite know that they can gain power by putting the selfish desires of the individual above that of the tribe even though the results are detrimental to the tribe as a whole. The liberals have consistently debased the religious morality of the local tribes and the country for political gain. For example, tribal morality and Christianity protects the life of the individual from conception. Traditionally, a woman would sacrifice her life for the life of the child for the sake of the preservation of the tribe. If a woman kills her children, the tribe would cease to exist. Yet the liberal movement celebrates the killing of unborn children. They have redefined the murder of an unborn child to *a woman's right to choose.* The purpose of the redefinition is to alleviate a woman's guilt of her decision to kill her child. The murder of a fetus does not benefit the tribe or society, but it relieves the woman of the responsibility of rearing her child.

---

[70] Epigenetics is the study of how the effects of an individual's life experiences can be passed down in the genetic code.

Liberals know they can buy the votes of the selfish, amoral masses if they replace traditional tribal cultural propagation with liberal public education. For example, liberal leaders have dumbed down education to justify the heinous crime of abortion. The liberal justification for killing an unborn child is that the fetus is a part of the mother and can therefore be eliminated like a wart or lipoma. The liberals teach that the fetus pops out of the uterus as an extension of the mother. Naïve brainwashed liberals have claimed that the belly button is evidence of the fact that a child is a part of a mother's body and justifies the women extricating her child as she would a mole. But a fetus is a living human being as any veracious high school biology course explains.

The fertilized egg, the zygote which possesses half the DNA of the mother and half of the father, is a free independent organism until implanted in the mother's uterus where after the ninth week *of life* it is called a fetus. The zygote is implanted in the uterus and receives nourishment from the woman. A fetus has its own brain, blood supply, and nervous system, and is no more a part of the mother than is a common parasite. Does a woman have the right to kill any parasite invading her body? Does she have the right to kill her child that depends on her for nourishment and life regardless of its age? Since more females are murdered in the womb than males, if the liberals truly wanted to protect *the rights of women*, they would outlaw abortions. No, indeed, they want to *buy* the votes of naïve, uneducated, lazy, selfish women with the lives of their children.

Abortion is just one example of how the liberals pervert religious morals for their benefit. There are many, but the mind-numbed liberal masses are sheltered from the social consequences of these liberal policies by their liberal leaders and liberal press and media. Liberal leaders are aware of these consequences since they have been discussed, described, and documented throughout history. Yet for the last fifty-plus years, they and their liberal henchmen in the press have intentionally hidden the facts. The masses are deceived and led to believe that the moral decay of society due to liberal policies is, in reality, progress toward a better, more just society for the voting masses. Liberal leaders know that dead babies can't vote.

GREED: CORPORATE AND GOVERNMENTAL

Corporate greed is a positive force in a capitalistic society. Corporate personhood includes greed as a manifestation of the natural personal greedy instincts that evolved during mankind's early evolution during times of scarce resources and intense competition. Corporate greed in an intensive competitive environment requires obtaining resources, utilizing resources, and producing a product or service at the lowest cost possible. The positive effect of corporate greed is that it causes intensive competition. Corporations, like people, have a wide range of abilities and, as in sports, maximum performance is achieved by having a fierce competitor. For example, sprinters running for the finish line, having someone just behind, will increase their efforts, perhaps even beyond their perceived abilities.

Just as a sprinter without competition will just coast over the finish line, a corporation in a monopolistic environment will not be motivated to achieve maximum efficiency. Thus, it is important in a complex capitalistic society to have intense competition between two or more corporations. Examples of two intense competitors are Pepsi Cola versus Coke Cola, Ford versus GM, Kellogg's versus General Mills, Visa versus MasterCard, and FedEx versus UPS, among others. This does not mean that there are not any other competitors to these companies (e.g., Dr. Pepper/7 Up, Chrysler, Quaker Oats, American Express), but the top two or three corporations dominate the field. In an environment such as this, government plays a major role in the regulation of corporate greed and has, for example, long ago outlawed monopolies and tries to prevent them today. But government is baroque, cumbersome, and has to be closely monitored. For example, currently, the Federal Communications Commission blocked the merger of AT&T with T-Mobile on the basis that eliminating a third party would reduce competition, while at the same time not objecting to Verizon obtaining more spectrum bandwidth. However, in the environment of limited resources (government-controlled bandwidth), it is equal access to the resource that enhances the competition and limits monopoly, not the number of companies involved. This action, in effect, is allowing Verizon—a dominant company—to become more so and reducing the effective competition in the field. The point is that the executive branch needs much closer scrutiny by the legislative branch than is currently the case.

Governments as well as corporations have personality and (corporate) greed applies to government as well as corporations, but there is very limited competition between governments. In the US, an individual can move from one city to another, one county to another, and even from one state to another to escape a corrupt or inefficient government, but it is difficult to move to a different country to escape a greedy federal government. With a powerful, effective government, corporate greed is not the problem, governmental incompetence and government greed is. The only control on an overreaching *democratic* government is the elected congress.

Many have lost confidence in the federal government and consider congress and the presidency as incompetent, ineffectual, corrupt, and subject to crony capitalism. They feel that individual members of congress are more interested in their personal gain than in monitoring the executive branch and working for the benefit of the populace as a whole. They feel that members of congress are corrupted by lobbyists and power brokers, that they use insider information to achieve gains in the stock market, and obtain sweetheart deals from government-connected entities to enhance their personal wealth. Moreover, they convert election funds intended for election expenses to their personal use. There is no effective federal authority to control such activities as congress rules itself, thus the need for a Congressional Incentive Amendment as given in Appendix A.

Intelligence

There are several types of intelligence: historical, social, and scientific, to mention but three important varieties. Excellence in one area does not portend excellence in the others.

Historical intelligence is that which allows us to remember the past and to relate the experiences of the past from one generation to the next. It accepts the past as the truth and does not question the source or reason for it. Social intelligence is the ability to control tribes, crowds, and individuals. It is the basic quality of leadership. Scientific knowledge is what our civilization is based on. It is the basis of engineering knowledge. In its first manifestation, it was how to build a fire, then how to grow grain. More recently, it is how to build cars, computers, and cell phones.

Scientific knowledge contains a reasoning, analytical component. Scientific knowledge and facts and their importance, change. In ancient times the Earth was *known* to be flat. Around the third century BC, astronomical observations established that it was spherical, but it remained until Magellan's circumnavigation to physically demonstrate the fact. Agricultural facts and knowledge are critical to human civilization, and engineering knowledge is critical in modern civilization. The ability to filter through a multitude of facts and determine which are true and which are relevant requires critical thinking.

Educators claim to teach students how to think, but memorizing facts and thinking are two quite different skills. Memorizing facts is the way information is passed from one generation to the next. It requires no active thinking process, just the acceptance that if a person of authority makes a claim, it must be true. Memorizing facts and responding to them impulsively results in a process akin to unreasoning instinct. Critical thinking is reasonable, reflective thinking that is aimed at deciding whether a *fact* is true, sometimes true, partly true, or false.

Effective critical thinking requires equal exposure to all schools of thought. If students are presented with only one side of a political philosophy, they do not have the tools to make an unbiased decision based on critical thinking. The liberal Ivy League schools purport to educate America's smartest students to be effective civil servants. But they are staffed with biased faculty and attract students that can absorb and regurgitate facts well. Neither faculty nor students can necessarily think critically. As a result, they are easily brainwashed with liberal social ideals, political goals, and ideology, and do not have the complete spectrum of political theory or skills required to engage in meaningful critical thinking.

Reasoning, Instinct, and Emotion

Reasoning is the ability to analyze new and existing information and consciously justify or change practices in response. Instinct is an instantaneous *unreasoning reaction. Emotion may also be unreasoning, but it implies a transition from a normal calm state to an emotional state of action.*

Every day we are flooded with emotions; some stronger than others, some more subtle. Do you like the color of this shirt? Does this skirt make me look fat? Emotions and instincts control a large portion of our lives, so it is important to understand the difference between instinct, emotion, and reasoning.

In an instinct, the reaction takes place before a transition from one emotional state to another can occur and indeed a transition is not even necessary. Reasoning and emotion are lacking in an instinctive reaction. Emotions and instinct often influence minor decisions like buying clothes, but major decisions are influenced, too.

Scientists have shown that information can be converted into instinctive action if repeated often enough. Not all information that is converted into instinct is based on fact. Much may be historical accounts, hearsay, rumor or just plain lies. Today, we are constantly being bombarded with the compassion and understanding of the liberals and the evil of the conservatives. The intent is to create an instinct to accept liberalism and reject conservatism by tying powerful emotional *positive* images to certain individuals and ideas and *negative* images to others.

Liberal propagandists have trained the mind-numbed masses to instinctively react negatively toward conservatives. When you first tell a liberal that you are conservative, their immediate reaction is "I don't agree with anything you say" if they are civil, or "I hate you" if they are not. You cannot reason with a liberal; they instinctively disagree with any point that does not agree with their propaganda. Reason is the basis of mathematics, science, technology, and commerce. It forms the foundation of questioning facts to determine the truth. It is the basic tool of conservatism. Propaganda is used to create biases and condition people to act instinctively to events. It is the basic tool of liberal political control.

PROPAGANDA

Propaganda is a form of communication that is aimed at influencing the attitude of a community toward some cause or position by presenting only one side of an argument. Propaganda is usually repeated and dispersed over a wide variety of media in order to create the chosen result in audience attitudes. Propaganda often presents facts selectively to encourage a particular synthesis, or uses loaded messages to produce an instinctual or emotional rather than rational response to the information presented. The desired result is a change of the attitude toward the subject in the target audience to further a political agenda. Propaganda can be used as a form of political warfare.
—Propaganda, *Wikipedia*

The liberals excel at propaganda. They have won the political propaganda war. They have emasculated the Republican and other conservative political parties not by better ideas or solutions but by constant propaganda. They present facts selectively. They lie openly and proudly. They use violent and abusive language with no repercussions. Propaganda trumps logic and reasoning and causes an instinctual emotional response.

Liberals have infiltrated and taken control of the nation's schools to brainwash our children. They have packed the major communication networks with liberals both visually and administratively so that only the liberal message is broadcast. They have convinced the government and the nation that an Ivy League education is superior to any other in the world. The Ivy League technique for winning an argument is not to present and discuss facts but to talk the fastest, loudest, and longest. Scientists have shown that this type of argumentation usually wins but it is usually wrong.

Liberals have taken control of the nation's schools of journalism so that they can redefine the American English language to their benefit. They have biased the terms capitalism, conservatism, racism, and Nazism. For example, Nazism has been branded as evil and morally corrupt and equated with conservative ideals without any analysis or understanding of the true nature of the term. Nazism was a complex social system with bad and good elements.

Via propaganda, liberals have adopted the repugnant, bad components of Nazism, while pinning a negative Nazi label on conservatives. Nazism is a form of socialism (Nazi is an acronym for National Socialist German Workers' Party). Liberals embrace national socialism, while conservatives reject it. Racism and classism, which socialists and liberals embrace, celebrate, and promote, were the Nazi excuses for the establishment of a superior race and the horrors of the Holocaust. Now liberals maintain their superiority. How long will it be before liberals call for the elimination their conservatives opponents? Just as the Russian, Chinese, Vietnamese, and Cambodians–socialists all–have done.

Nazism favored private property, freedom of contract, and promoted the creation of a national identity—positive concepts that conservatives embrace and liberals reject. In summary, by using Nazi propaganda techniques, liberals have managed to embrace the evils of Nazism rejected by conservatives, while at the same time convince the public that the conservatives are the real evil ones.

CLASSICAL CLASSISM

Liberalism, socialism, and communism, like all forms of totalitarianism, use the classism instinct to achieve power and control the tribe.

The instinctual classist structure of society evolved from the primitive patriarchal tribal social structure. In primitive times, tribal existence depended on the oldest, strongest dominant male leading the tribe through hostile surroundings, with competing tribes searching for the limited resources necessary for life. To assure that his talents would survive to lead the tribe in the next generation, the patriarch favored his sons, family members, and friends. He assured that they had the best food, water, and shelter, optimizing the chances that the family genes would be passed on.

Like the dominant male in all herding species, the patriarch had to spend considerable effort defending his position and keeping the other men in line. He maintained order among his cohorts by chastising and punishing the men that were out of line but doling out kindness and favors to those that toed the mark. Men could climb the ranks of the social system by respecting the higher authorities and winning their friendship and, eventually, with cunning, skill, deviousness, and luck become the patriarch themselves.

Again, like most herding animals, not only was there a pecking order among the men in a tribe, but among their families and even individuals within extended families. In times of limited resources, the highest ranking and their direct descendants had access to the choice food and shelter. The lower ranking were forced to make do with what they could find. Social hierarchy was passed down with rank. It was not based on an individual's skills or abilities. The off-spring of leaders were considered leaders, while the offspring of sub-ordinates were considered subordinate, so that the children of the higher ranking men would be given considerable leeway, even to the extent of wasting, without any repercussions, the precious resources that others needed.

As populations grew and tribal interactions became more com-plex, this primitive pecking order evolved into the class-based sys-tem of dynastic kingdoms. The passing down of social rank became the class-based system of Europe and elsewhere. The leaders became kings not by skill but by birth. The familial relatives and cohorts became the peerage and ruling classes. The *subordinates* became the serfs and peasants. Eventually, the subordinates became nothing more than property and a means for satisfying the needs of the ruling classes. Even the lives of the subordinates had little merit in them-selves and were forfeit for the benefit of the royalty's desire to achieve more power by taking resources from competing tribal kingdoms. European history is replete with conflicts between these extended tribes. As technology advanced, these conflicts became more and more violent, culminating in the world wars of the twentieth century.

All socialistic philosophies (i.e., liberalism, socialism, commu-nism, etc.) are descended from the classist line of tribal organization. None of these movements are truly egalitarian. They are basically the replacement of one ruling class by another. Communist leaders, Nazi leaders, and modern liberal leaders all put themselves above the com-mon people. Liberal leaders consider themselves to be the equivalent of the European ruling classes. They feel that they are above every-one else, that they know what is best for everyone, and that because of their *social status* they deserve better than anyone else. They take from the hardworking lower classes and give to their favored classes to get and maintain power so that they can enrich themselves and their offspring. They feel they can do anything to achieve and main-tain their power. Witness the Nazi genocide, the Russian gulag, Mao's giant leap forward, and the killing fields in Cambodia. The overconfident arrogance of liberals is destructive and ultimately leads to *wars, financial disasters, and collapsed civilizations.*[71]

Today's liberal leaders are no different. Their goal is to establish and maintain a classist society at any expense, with the liberal ruling class on top. Liberals politically kill their opponents with lies, distortions, and a compliant press, but the liberals' most powerful weapon to maintain power is redistribution. In liberal philosophy, there is a limited amount of resources which must be redistributed to maintain their power and control. The royal classes of Europe distributed land and bound servants to their loyal minions. They gave economic favors such as trade fair licenses to their favorite feudal lords, in effect, pioneering the practice of crony capitalism. Liberal politicians distribute money—the limited resource in an industrial society—to their favored subclasses for votes and to their favored industries in return for political loyalty and campaign contribution kickbacks. They have no compunction about destroying the American egalitarian society to establish and maintaining their classist society.

---

[71] Veronique Greenwood. *Discover*. January 2, 2012, p. 54.

Classism and Racism in America

"All men are created equal."
—The Declaration of Independence

The most important component of the American culture is the rejection of the ruling class, the European class-based society, and classes in general. The Declaration of Independence was not simply a statement against the political domination of America by Britain, but against the entire European classist society. European society was, at the time of the Revolution, dominated by an all-powerful ruling class that claimed that their power was derived from God and that the *rights* of the lesser classes were derived from the whims of the ruling class. Much of the world still is dominated by class-based societies. The rejection of a ruling class is basic to American culture.

Freedom, another component of the American culture, is not truly possible in a classist society. Freedom means being able to do anything you want to do that doesn't harm anybody else. Classism restricts the actions of the individuals based on their class. Serfs were not allowed to fight in wars. Noblemen would not plow fields or sow grain. In some societies, it is demeaning for some classes to clean up after themselves as that is a job for a *lower*-class individual. And while many liberals would claim that present-day Europe is *classless*, in Britain and many other countries, there still is a celebrated royalty and an underlying class-based society. There is a distinction between butler and master, between members of the peerage and commoners.

The word of someone in nobility is likely to be given more credence than some local fellow on the street.

Conservatives support the idea of dynamic tribal membership—in essence, dynamic merit-based classes. One is not born into a class, but is able to join and exit classes at will. But the individuals must demonstrate that they want to become a member of the new class or tribe or they may be rejected. They demonstrate their desire by the way they dress, the way they act, the way they speak, the language they speak, in general, the way they live (i.e.,the culture they affect). Conservatives believe that these features are the important determinant of a person's class.

The one feature people cannot affect is their race. Racism and its various manifestations are due to fundamental, primitive tribal instincts. Racial distinctions were important in primitive societies as it provided the ability of a tribal member to make an instinctive judgment about strangers, such as to which tribe they belong and whether they are to be befriended or feared. In the inter-tribal hostile environment of the last 50,000 years, instinctive reaction to race and other physical evidence of *differentness* was often the difference between life and death. Without racism—the immediate recognition that someone is *different*—different tribes would not have evolved. It is the mechanism that allows a tribe to exist and dominate, even eliminate competitive tribes. Racism, as practiced by liberalism, is the worst kind of classism.

Like all instincts, racism can be conditioned. By and large, in conservative American society today, racism, like classism, has been subdued. This is not to say that race is not noticed, only that after an initial recognition of race, a stranger's worth is measured more by dress, language, and mannerisms than his physical features. Racism is amoral. It is not immoral in and of itself, but, like all instincts, it can be used for immoral purposes. Unfortunately, today, liberals constantly use race for class distinction to get power and control over people for their own personal gain. To the degree that racism harms others or raises one class over another, it is contrary to traditional egalitarian American culture. Racism and multiculturalism are liberal mechanisms to divide Americans into different, distinct, competing, even warring, classes. Instead of the traditional conservative American *e pluribus Unum* melting pot philosophy of equality and integration, the liberal political philosophy is to divide and conquer by competing blacks against whites, whites against Latinos, Latinos against Asians, rich against poor, urban against rural, and on and on and on.

PROGRESSIVE LIBERALS

Progressive liberals are socialists and believe that all the people of the world are of one tribe. They believe that the tribal ruling class system that evolved over the millennia should be applied to the world as a whole—a new world order."

Progressive liberals, or simply liberals, believe that there is one ruling class that knows instinctively what is best for the other classes, and therefore that it should control the world. For example, the tribal instinct of helping those in need applied to the world means that individuals anywhere in the world, regardless of tribal affiliation that have *excess wealth*, are obligated by tribal instinct to help those individuals anywhere in the world that are in need. Their mantra is "Give your fair share according to your ability or take governmental welfare regardless of your need." This is the rationale behind the liberals and President Obama's effort to weaken American culture and power.

The retrograde pseudo-intellectual liberals have weakened American culture consistently over the last one hundred years. Their goal is to reestablish the class-based European social structure where an all-powerful ruling class determines the future of the dependent lower classes. The Ivy League schools idealize the European culture and intentionally educate the nation's *smartest students* to become ruling class bureaucrats and politicians. The result is a de facto ruling class that arrogantly self-proclaims its intellectual superiority, giving them the right, even the obligation, to control the lower classes' life at the cost of their freedom.

One recent example of the liberal's goal to establish a new world order is the United Nations' Arms Trade Treaty. ATT is the first step down the slippery slope to negate America's Second Amendment to the Constitution. The treaty calls for worldwide registration of firearms so that they then can be confiscated as has been historically done in all socialist countries. The liberals of the new world order believe that by disarming America but empowering the world community, Americans can be forced to distribute their *undeserved excessive share* of the world's limited wealth to the rest of the world.

The liberals justify this stance to themselves and their minions by declaring that they are smarter than anyone else, and that the social good is enhanced by *elevating* the poor out of poverty and other social goals which they themselves define and redefine to meet their political needs. But their real goal is to establish themselves as the ruling class so that they can exempt themselves from the laws they pass and reap the rewards of political control and corruption. It is by no accident that Washington D.C. and surrounding areas have become the most prosperous in the nation. For the last one hundred years, prosperity followed economic development. Now it follows liberal political power.

CONSERVATISM

American conservatism is based on small dynamic tribes competing with one another in a free, technological-based laissez-faire capitalist society. Conservatives strive for a world unencumbered with a ruling class. A free, industrious world with free worldwide trade would increase the total amount of resources sufficiently to bring prosperity to all.

There was a resurgence of the original primitive tribal instincts of freedom and self-reliance with the founding of America. These original tribal instincts rejected the ruling class-based instincts that evolved in Europe and elsewhere over the last 5,000 to 10,000 years, and when fused with science, technology, and laissez-faire capitalism, produced the highest standard of living the world has ever known. Freedom, self-reliance, and responsibility are the bases of American capitalism and conservatism.

In American capitalism, small dynamic tribes are allowed to pop into existence, compete with one another, and die if unsuccessful. Those tribes that satisfy societal needs most effectively and efficiently persist whether they are a company, a church, or a social organization. Dynamic tribes, like individuals, may act in concert with some tribes and in conflict with others. For example, social tribes often work cooperatively to help the needy and for the good of their constituents, while business tribes are competitive and strive to eliminate their opponents.

Laissez-faire capitalism and free markets allow the primitive selfish hostile instincts to be expressed in a civilized manner. The primitive instinct to eliminate, even kill, competing tribes is sublimated to simply driving the opposition out of business. The result is the most effective, efficient, peaceful system for communicating and satisfying the needs of billions of consumers. Serendipitously, the excess resources produced by this laissez-faire system allow the social tribal organizations to provide for the needs of the poor and helpless.

In American conservatism, every business, every church, every social organization, even ideally every government, functions as a small tribe. In a small tribe, the communication between the rulers and the ruled is intimate and approximates the environment in which the original tribal instincts evolved. Freedom is essential so that individuals can choose to belong to as many tribes as needed to fulfill their needs.

In conservatism, the government is the only tribal organization to which one belongs that is not voluntary and accordingly must be limited in its duties. Among these duties are inter-tribal (i.e., inter-state and international) defense and the responsibility to regulate and monitor the interaction of the dynamic tribes which provide for economic and social needs. Because of the monopoly that government holds on the people, it must be kept small so that it can effectively communicate directly with the people.

LIBERALS VERSUS CONSERVATIVES

Liberals and conservatives possess the same sets of instincts, morals, values, and emotions, but they have different approaches for dealing with them. The conflict between liberalism and conservatism is a war of tribal cultural evolution. The new conservative social structure is battling the old liberal classist one. This is not a war that will be won with one battle. In fact, the conflict has been simmering for thousands of years, but a major battle was won over two hundred years ago with the fleeing from an enslaving, socialist, classist Europe and the founding of a free, capitalistic American culture.

Liberals feel that in large populations, satisfying the basic tribal social needs—caring for children, sharing with the poor, helping the sick—can best be done with an all-powerful government in an elitist, classist social structure. Conservatives feel that individuals interacting in multiple small social groupings is more akin to the original tribal environment of freedom and personal responsibility and is more rewarding and effective.

Liberals feel it is the duty of the more productive members of the tribe to share the rewards of their efforts with the others. Since the world is just one tribe and there is only one planet, there are fixed resources that must be shared equally. It is the duty of the elite liberal ruling class to provide for the welfare of the poor everywhere. Thus, while the big government liberals complain that the rich classes are not paying their *fair share* to provide for the social needs, the conservatives see a faceless system of legal stealing called taxation put in place to satisfy the wants of the lower classes in exchange for their vote. Liberals achieve this goal by appealing to the lower classes' insecurity and lazy, selfish instincts. Conservatives see a system where the lazy, who could spend time contributing to the welfare of the tribe, do not do so because the government will provide for them; the stingy who could afford to give to charity do not do so because *the rich* are going to pay their share for them; the politicians who could earn an honest living in a different occupation, prefer to live off the corruption inherent in big government. That is, the liberal *fair share* call is a code phrase for saying the government will *make others pay more so I can get away with doing and paying less to society and keeping more for myself.*

The conservatives feel that individuals and small social charitable organizations and groups such as churches, the United Way, the YMCA, Habitat for Humanity, etc. are much more effective at serving social needs. A system of small efficient social organizations that mimic a tribal environment where everyone knows everyone and is aware of everyone's needs is best. Conservatives believe that there is merit in work and that there is an instinctual need to contribute to society and that the satisfaction for doing so and the reward for giving is sufficient motivation for the small tribal system to work. The liberals complain that that may be true, but conservatives still do not do enough. There are many social needs that are not taken care of by such organizations. The conservatives counter that it is the liberal's personal responsibility to fulfill these needs and that their time is better spent doing so than in forcing *the rich* to pay for their responsibilities so that they have more time to play golf.

The conflict between the liberals and conservatives is a conflict due to the replacement of the old monolithic tribal fixed class social structure of the liberals with the new freedom-based, egalitarian, dynamic multi-tribal organization of the conservatives. To a conservative, tribal membership is not based on race, color, or other inherited physical characteristics, but on language, dress, and attitude. Class membership is of little merit. The status in a tribe depends mostly on how hard one works and lives. To a liberal, there is but one global, universal tribe with numerous classes that are determined by location of birth (e.g., flyover country versus the coasts), race, inheritance, and social status. Class membership determines your role in life and is determined at your birth and cannot be changed. The liberal elite class is always on top.

The problem with the liberal philosophy is that tribal instincts evolved over tens of thousands of years in an environment of small groups of people with close interpersonal communication. It took thousands of generations for this initial small tribal culture to develop into the class-based system which accommodated tribes of thousands and even hundreds of thousands. Liberals want to maintain these old tribal instincts and methods and apply them to the modern world. Sufficient time has not elapsed to allow the evolution of a primitive tribal culture based on the close communication in a tribe of a few hundred to be effectively applied to tribes of millions and billions. An alternative system, conservative laissez-faire capitalism and free trade, is evolving as the only viable approach for working with billions of people.

In conservatism, government is the only tribal organization to which one belongs that is not voluntary. For this reason, our Founding Fathers designed our governments to serve at the pleasure of the people. In a free conservative culture, people are free to choose governments by relocating. It is common to select a community in which to live based on local taxes and government services such as schools. Even state governments can be selected by moving as reflected by companies and individuals fleeing high tax states for more responsible governments. However, changing national governments is much more difficult. Our forefathers understood this and established a minimal national government and reserved all unspecified powers to the states.

The National Government

"Several critical ingredients are required for a good political order among them are a strong state, the rule of law, a means for holding rulers to account for their actions, a merit-based (non-aristocratic) military leadership, sophisticated taxation, and a bureaucracy based on ability rather than family [or college] [72] connection."
—The Origins of Political Order [73]

Our founding fathers were successful in establishing a national government that met many of Mr. Fukuyama's criteria ('The Origins of Political Order'). His book also notes that there is a "hardwired human tendency to make ties of kinship the primary criterion for conferring wealth, power, and status," and that there is an inverse correlation between the strength of the centralized state and the strength of patrimonial groups. He is echoing the effects of a ruling class-based society. Unfortunately, over the last seventy-five years, our leaders have led us into the trap of establishing a governing class based on birth and ideology which exempts itself from the effects of the laws it demands the *lower classes* obey.

We are a tribal species composed of numerous sub-tribes. Tribes and sub-tribes grow, evolve, and die. But there is one sub-tribe that

---

[72] The author's addition.

[73] Francis Fukuyama. "The Origins of Political Order: From Prehuman Times to the French Revolution." Farrar, Status and Giroux. New York, 2011.

never dies—the government. Indeed, many would propose that it should. The national government has grown into an organization that is out of control. As a super-tribe being, it exhibits all of the antisocial behavior of primitive tribes that fought for existence in a hostile environment. For example, self-preservation—it will never kill itself for a better good; hoarding—it always needs more money and more people; laziness—it only produces the minimal amount of services necessary to exist; and aggression—the desire to take, violently if necessary, resources that it wants from the population it is supposed to serve. This monstrous beast is promoted and cultivated by our political leaders.

In order to feed this beast, the *big government* class exploits our instincts. When they communicate via their willing minions in the media a message indicating a tribal need, we instinctively respond in the manner they desire. Using our instinctual fear of poverty and sickness, they *induce* us to *share* our wealth so that the government can help the needy, the children, and the infirm. Unfortunately, many of the instincts, such as racism and retribution which they use that evolved during primitive tribal life, are antisocial and are the root of yesterday's international and today's inter-cultural warfare.

The national governments are the only tribal subspecies with no outside control other than other governments. We, as a species, are only now learning how to control governments peacefully, but the process is very slow because it is based on instinctual evolution over generations. Logic, thought, and reason, as applied to social issues, are relatively new evolutionary features possessed by few individuals and by even fewer *newsmen*, making them easy to manipulate. As a result, logic loses out to the more primitive tribal instincts. The only peaceful controls on government are our leaders, but unfortunately our national leaders are more interested in furthering their own primitive instinctual selfish personal goals than in benefiting the nation.

Why and How Liberal Politicians Lie

Liberal politicians use fear to control us. Conservative politicians use logic to persuade us.

Fear is a very strong primitive emotion rooted in a very primitive part of our brain. Evolution has resulted in us reacting instinctively to fear. Fear is one of the most primal and enduring of all the emotions. It plays tricks with our memory and our perception of reality. It can cause reactions to events without *remembering* why. If we have an innate fear of an object or situation, we can be conditioned to be afraid of another object or situation if the two are associated with each other. This conditioned fear is one of the most useful techniques that natural selection has developed to increase the survival odds of organisms in an unpredictable environment. It is the primary mechanism that politicians use to influence our vote and maintain control over us.

There are two ways the brain reacts to fear. One is conscious and rational; the other is unconscious and instinctive. The conscious rational system forms associations with past experiences and the current situation and requires a few seconds to react. The unconscious instinctive mechanism alerts the body to potential danger and initiates an unthinking reaction in only a fraction of a second.

The instinctive reaction is of obvious benefit in a hostile world, but it must be learned or conditioned. The situations to fear are not innately known since they depend on the environment. In order to accommodate the wide variety of dangerous situations, evolution has designed our brain to be conditioned to threats by our peers, parents, and elders. These threats may be physical such as bears, spiders, fire, and hostile tribes, or sociological such as fear of being rejected or abandoned. Once learned, these fear responses are very difficult to eradicate. The brain is designed to allow the instinctual fear system to take quick action in threatening situations. It overrides and prevents the slower conscious awareness—thinking response system—from taking action.

Our primitive tribal instincts cause us to accept the statements of our parents, elders, and leaders without question. We inherently trust them to warn us of dangers and tell us the truth. Unfortunately, political leaders use this inherent trust in them to repeatedly associate a perceived sign of danger with a stressful situation so that the whole autonomic response system is activated over and over. This brainwashing creates a feedback loop that physically reinforces the emotional reaction in the brain so that on cue our instinctive fear system will respond favorably to their political wishes without thinking.

To experience the effect of this brainwashing firsthand, reveal to one of your liberal friends with whom you have had a pleasant platonic nonpolitical relationship that you are a conservative. Their brainwashed instinctive reaction is to step back and regard you with fear. Then they will instinctively say that they do not believe in anything you believe in. If you can maintain the relationship and can actually get them to discuss issues calmly, you and they will find that you have much common ground, such as politicians lie and are corrupt and that everyone wants to help the poor and elderly. There is just a disagreement on how best to address the issues. It is the trained unreasoning instinctive response to fear that liberal politicians use to get the *mind-numbed masses* to vote for them without thinking about the issues or the validity of the proposed solutions.

Our brain takes charge of assessing the emotional intensity of both pleasant and unpleasant situations. The human body does not function very well in the presence of negative emotions, but it works exceptionally well when emotions are positive. People naturally try to overcome their negative feelings with positive emotions.

Politicians use this natural phenomenon by creating or reviewing a negative situation, and then assuring us that their solution will result in a positive result. Thus, when a stressful situation is presented, such as a mass murder by an armed gunman, the fear circuitry steers us toward the politicians' *positive action* of eliminating guns. The fear circuitry propels us in directions that are not always rational. The real threat of violence is from emotionally unstable suicidal people who desperately seek society's recognition, not guns.

Liberal politicians influence our instinctual responses by repeatedly associating a seemingly positive but frequently ineffectual response to a negative emotion. Take, for example, the threats of gun violence and the national debt. Liberal politician know their *solutions* are emotional and ineffectual, for if they actually solved the problems, they would lose the issues as control mechanisms.

Conservative politicians believe their solutions are well-thought-out and reasoned, not emotional. Unfortunately, the brain is designed to allow the instinctive fear system to take quick instinctive responses in threatening situations. It overrides and prevents the slower conscious awareness—thinking response system—from taking action. As a result, liberals win elections and conservatives lose.

WHY EPIGENETICS IS IMPORTANT

Recently, biologists have discovered a method of non-DNA species change which can be passed on to subsequent generations.

Biologists that study genetics have discovered a method of species change called epigenetics. Epigenetics refers to modifications to the genome that are not caused by a change in the DNA but by biological processes which take place during cell division and which can then be passed on by cell division in the individual and even on to subsequent generations.

Normally, these changes are *random* and cancel each other out, but in technophysio evolution,[74] if a large majority of members of the species change the environment in the same way, this change can be passed down to subsequent generations. If the subsequent generations experience the same environmental situation for a sufficient number of generations, the change can become *permanent*. Children raised in an environment tend to perpetuate it and propagate it. A few generations ago, taking a handout from the government was considered shameful, but liberals have changed culture via epigenetics to where today it is considered a right.

The ruling class liberals realize that a majority of people are willing to sacrifice freedom for security, so they are using government to

---

[74] The field of technophysio evolution addresses how the human body expresses itself over the generations in response to technology and work.

change society via epigenetics for their selfish benefits. For example, they use the fear of poverty and the unknown to push through social programs, such as social security and the war on poverty. These laws modify the environment for multiple generations resulting in the modification of the American human genome to expect government to provide security. The need to provide one's own security via hard work, churches, and social organizations is seemly replaced by government *largess* but, in reality, at the loss of freedom.

Today, we are experiencing the modification of our society to accept the murder of the defenseless and useless. The liberals are pushing the murder of the unborn for the convenience of the careless, irresponsible unmarried women and men. Once the principle that lives that are inconvenient can be terminated has been established, the liberals will establish death panels to determine economic impact of medical attention and if we should be allowed to live or die.

Then the liberals will progress to eliminating those who disagree with them as in all totalitarian socialist societies like the communists in Russia, China, Cambodia, and elsewhere have done.

The outrage of this progression is the destruction of the free egalitarian American society which has produced the most advanced, most prosperous society in human history to be replaced by a classist, racist, socialist culture. The political elite who make these modifications to society exempt themselves from their mandates. The political elite wants to set up a society whereby they and their progeny are the rightful political parasites of the other classes.

SECTION 3

How to Restore the American Dream

The unique American culture can only be restored by eliminating the political elite class. Debt limits and term limits won't work, only restricting congressional income to the median income will have a lasting effect.

The freedom-based democratic institutions upon which our country was founded have been greatly weakened. Obamacare is the epitome of congress run amuck. Laws are voted on and passed that the members of congress do not read or understand and the populace does not want. In order to impose his liberal paradise, Obama established himself as the de facto king of the country, deciding what laws should be enforced and which should be ignored. Obama was well on the way to achieving the liberals' goal of destroying the American way of life. Liberals, like their leftist communist and Nazi brethren, will result to any extreme, including violence, to achieve their end result. In the last political cycle, Democrats and their union minions demonstrated in Wisconsin and elsewhere their disrespect for the rule of law and their inclination toward violence. If the liberal agenda is not stopped, the ultimate result will be violent revolution and warfare. The liberals have won the class-based battle for the minds of the low information, mind-numbed, non-thinking, self-serving masses. A new front in the war for maintaining the American way of life must be opened—an Article V Constitutional Convention.

The road to liberal political domination is based on using fear and primitive racist instinct to divide the population into multiple antagonistic classes: black versus white, Latinos versus whites, Asians versus whites, Republicans versus Democrats, conservatives versus liberals, men versus women, rich versus poor, and on and on. There is, however, a flaw in the liberal stratagem. Their approach to obtaining power depends on perverting the unique American culture. The Pledge of Allegiance—"one Nation under God with liberty and justice for all"—and the motto on the seal of the United States—"*e pluribus Unum*"—identifies the country's goal as uniting the people and their various cultural heritages into one culture, one language, one people, one country, one class. Aunt Eller in Rodgers and Hammerstein's Oklahoma sums up the fundamental American egalitarian principle: "I ain't better than anybody else, but I'll be damned if I not just as good!" The liberal mistake is in establishing class rivalry as their main political tool and at the same time setting themselves up as the ruling class nobility. An elite ruling class is the one class mistrusted and scorned by all. All of the *lower* classes will support a constitutional amendment which takes the money and power out of Washington and away from the ruling class. The conservative talk shows, tea party, and other grassroots organizations must lead the way to organizing an Article V Convention to accomplish the task.

A powerful liberal nanny state government is not wanted or needed. Unfettered by inherited birth class limitations and free to take advantage of the opportunities offered by capitalism, persistent, hardworking, self-respecting people have fulfilled their American dream. Having achieved their goals, Americans traditionally share their bounty directly with the less fortunate in their community, not through the *largess* of a self-serving governing class but via their local tribal organizations. Immigrants have come from all over the world to escape the limitations imposed upon them by their classist, racist, corrupt governments to join the unique free egalitarian charitable American culture—to become an American.

Rebuffed by the American culture, the self-proclaimed intellectually superior *royal* class aristocracy, fomented by their selfishness, greed, and avarice, has endeavored for over one hundred years to destroy the American culture and reinstate their class-based system. They claim to be *progressive* but indeed they are retrogressive in their efforts to reestablish the European socialist birth class system modeled on the ancient medieval concept of the sovereign authority of a ruling class headed by a king. The purported intent of royalty and the liberals is to improve the living standard of the poor to create a more equal society. The actuality is the establishment of an elite class who govern not for the citizenry but for themselves.

During the 2012 election, the Republican Party demonstrated itself to be completely ineffectual against the liberal Democrat propaganda machine. Many Republican leaders are complicit in this greed for graft and power. The policy of the Republican Party of being Democrat *lite* only substantiates the corrupt liberal ideals and facilitates the liberal slide to depravity. The only hope for the unique American culture to revive and survive is to remove the money and political corruption from our nation's government. Liberals rail against the *rich* one percent while at the same time establishing themselves as the all-powerful one ten-thousandth of one percent. They vote themselves extravert salaries, benefits, and extract bribery, graft, and favors from constituents, unions, lobbyists, and businesses. All non-politicians, liberals, conservatives, Democrats, and Republicans alike disdain the political ruling class and agree that congress must be reined in. It is impossible to restore traditional American values without a significant change in the national government. Regardless of whether the future is liberal, socialist, conservative, or capitalist, congress should serve the people and, as their reward, receive the thanks of the American people and the knowledge that they made a difference. They should expect no more or no less compensation or benefits than their laws and decisions provide for the general population. A corrupt, cowering congress will not change its ways, only an Article V Convention run by the states has the power to reset congress and reestablish the American dream.

Action must be taken while most of the individual states are still governed by Americans with traditional American values and principles. The states must use the Constitution's Article V process to limit federal power and reinforce states' rights. The American Legislative

Exchange Council (www.alec.org) has a Web page devoted to how to proceed. The ALEC literature rightly points out that it is important for the states to describe the problem(s) the convention is to address, not the solution. It is the job the of convention delegates to discuss solutions and propose amendments that then must be ratified by the states.

There are many problems that might be appropriate for calling for an Article V convention. Figure 1 reiterates the problems identified in section 1. Some other problems are 1) balancing the national budget, 2) reinforcing the Second Amendment, 3) illegal immigration, 4) imposing federal mandates on the individual states, 5) limiting the duration of Supreme Court appointments, and 6) strengthening the impeachment process.

Addressing these points, first, some method of preventing unbridled spending would promote a more prosperous future, but caution must be exercised to allow deficit spending in times of national emergency, such as war or economic collapse. Second, the Supreme Court has allowed the Second Amendment to be greatly weakened. Additional language should be added to prevent an overbearing federal government from dominating the people by use of armed force. For example, the national guard of the states should have its first allegiance to the state and can only be called up by the federal government with the acquiesce of the state. Third, the problem of illegal immigration is primarily one of not enforcing existing laws. Congress needs the power to impeach members of the executive branch for non-execution of duty, such as not enforcing laws passed by Congress. Fourth, except in the areas of national security and defense, the Supremacy Clause should be weakened. For example, all states should have the right to refuse to participate in a federal program forced upon them. The federal taxes proposed for such a program would be forfeit back to the state. Fifth, limiting Supreme Court appointments to ten years would maintain the court's independence but would allow for less effective judges to be replaced. Sixth, as mentioned in the third point, expanding the power of impeachment would restore some balance of power between the executive and legislative branches.

Given these many problems, it is difficult to address them all in one constitution convention. The ALEC literature suggests that an Article V Convention be limited to one critical issue. The Magna Carta was the first step in restricting the unlimited power of the ruling classes in England. An Article V Convention should be the first step in restricting the unlimited power of the liberal class in America. Congress has shown itself to be ineffectual in addressing this issue itself. Congress has stood by while the liberal class has modified the Constitution via executive directives and Supreme Court decision against the will of the people.

It is the thesis of this book that a constitutional amendment that eliminates corruption and supports individuals who want to serve their country rather than be a professional politician should be the primary focus of an Article V Convention. Congressional corruption can be checked by limiting a congressman's absolute income to the median non-government income of the congressman's congressional district. Absolutely no other sources of income or benefits for the members of congress or their families would be allowed. The intent is that a citizens' congress dedicated to the public good, not obtaining personal wealth, would address the many issues mentioned in this book. For example, they could address the national debt by slightly reducing or holding federal spending constant. Unfettered by hordes of moneyed lobbyists anxious to distribute their wealth, they could simplify tax laws. They could institute common sense health reform laws. They could pass immigration reform. Since they will benefit or suffer directly from the laws they pass, they would be willing to revisit legislation that did not turn out as anticipated. A suggested amendment intended to limit congressional income is given in Appendix A and is replicated at income-equality-amendment.org.

The TV, radio, and print media must lead the state governments through the process for calling an Article V convention and explain the need to the state governments and the people. Currently, the conservative media are as ineffectual as the Republicans when it comes to actually combating the liberal problem. The conservative commentators complain and shake their heads at the biased liberal media and RINO Republicans. Some have been *complaining* and explaining the situation for almost forty years to no effect. Indeed, the conservative media is doing more harm than good because the constant repetition of the liberal biases and lies only reinforces them in the minds of the low information voters. If the conservative media is sincerely interested in the well-being of the American people, it must generate the grassroots support necessary for changing the political system. Otherwise, they are just as morally corrupt and hypocritical as the liberal politicians in that they are making obscene money off the demise of the American dream instead of defending and working to preserve it. An aggressive posture by the conservative media will give the state governments the courage to call for an Article V Convention to control congress. Only an amendment that prevents congress from exempting themselves from the laws of the land and limits their income to that of the working man will free the country from a corrupt, liberal-dominated government and congress.

1) Prevent the overpowering national government from dominating local governments (p. 24);

2) Need politicians that can think and do what is best for the nation, not make instinctual decisions that are best for themselves (pp. 28 and 44);

3) The national government should not be involved in debates involving tribal intelligence (p. 32);

4) Personal communication by any means—verbal, US mail, email, Facebook, Twitter, or cell phone—needs to be clearly protected in the Constitution (p. 34);

5) Clarification of the First Amendment and the role of the press and the media is essential (p. 36);

6) Classism has no place in the American culture (p. 42);

7) Must prohibit the use of classism and racism in laws and edicts (p. 47);

8) Eminent domain should be severely restricted (p. 50);

9) Education is the responsibility of the local government (p. 52);

10) Restore the duties of the state, local, and regional governments by reestablishing states' rights (p. 58);

11) A national consumption tax is the only reasonable tax in an environmentally sensitive capitalistic society (p. 62);

12) An Article V Constitution Convention is the only way to circumvent the liberal mentality instilled by the media, educators, and politicians (p. 69);

13) The constitution must prohibit any law that favors one class over another, whether the class division is based on race, economic status, social status, health, or any other criteria (p. 75);

14) Need a constitutional provision that prevents elected officials from exempting themselves from the laws they pass (p. 78);

15) Fix congresspersons' income to their constituents' median income (p. 81);

16) Amend the Constitution so that politicians are rewarded for the laws they pass in the same manner and degree as their constituents (p. 85); and

17) Limit the federal Supremacy Clause by allowing states to opt out of any federal program and have the money collected from the state for the program to be returned directly to the state (p. 88).

Issues Affecting Our Freedom

Figure 1

APPENDIX A

The Congressional Incentive Amendment

Whereas the U.S. Government's authority is derived from the people;

Whereas the primary function of Congress is to provide for the welfare of the people;

Whereas the members of Congress are in a position of service, responsibility, and duty, not enrichment;

Therefore any burden borne by the people shall be borne equally by the members of Congress as follows.

The sole source of compensation for the members of Congress shall be based on the median hourly compensation of the people; calculated as follows:

One half of the hourly compensation shall be equal to one half of the median hourly compensation of the congressman's non-governmental constituents' district, and one half of the hourly compensation shall be equal to one half of the median hourly compensation of the United States non-governmental citizenry as a whole. The congressman's hourly compensation shall be updated yearly.

Total yearly compensation shall be based solely on the number of hours worked in that year. The number of hours worked shall be based on the number of hours Congress is in session, with a quorum as stated in Article I of the Constitution. Hourly compensation includes all sources of income and benefits both current and future; including, but not limited to, direct compensation, health care, retirement benefits, including all governmental benefits such as social security, Medicare, educational benefits, travel expenses, office expenses, etc. All other funds, gifts, and contributions, whether received directly or indirectly by the congressman, are the property of the federal government. Such funds must be judiciously husbanded and surrendered to the government on departure from office. Specifically, campaign funds are the property of the government.

Upon election, all of the assets of a congressman, except for a residence in his home district, shall be put in a blind trust. Upon departure from congress, the congressman's assets shall be returned, in kind, increased in value by the same percentage the congressman's median hourly compensation increased during the congressman's tenure.

All acquaintances and all relatives of members of Congress that are third cousins or closer as determined by the Canon Law Relationship Chart, either by blood, sanctified marriage, or common law marriage, employed by the congressman either directly or indirectly, or employed by the government are subject to the Congressional Incentive Amendment rules regardless of their position.

This amendment shall take effect immediately upon passage and apply to all living members of Congress, retroactively.

A Congressional Incentive Monitoring Branch of government shall be set up by the Executive Branch, but populated by the state governments solely for implementing and monitoring compliance to this amendment. The compensation of the members of the Congressional Incentive Monitoring Branch shall be the same as Congress's, including benefits, except: 1) any monetary penalties incurred by congressmen, 2) any hourly compensation due to any congressman removed from office due to this amendment, and 3) the calculated hourly compensation normally earned by any congressman serving prison time due to violation of this amendment shall be added to the compensation of the members of the Congressional Incentive Monitoring Branch.

Members of the Congressional Incentive Monitoring Branch may be removed by a two-thirds majority vote of the U.S. Supreme Court. Any Congressional Incentive Monitoring Branch Members removed by the U.S. Supreme Court will lose all of their benefits.

Violations of this amendment as determined by the Congressional Incentive Monitoring Branch results in automatic removal from office and a mandatory penalty of the maximum of 1) one year in jail and a fine equivalent to one year of congressional compensation, or 2) the median U.S. penalty for equivalent offenses. No member of Congress shall receive any income while in violation of this amendment or while serving sentences due to violation of this amendment.

Failure to implement the Congressional Incentive Monitoring Branch of government within one year of passage of this amendment is an automatic violation of this amendment and all elected members of the Executive Branch shall be determined guilty and punished as specified above by the Legislative Branch. Failure of the Legislative Branch to fulfill their responsibility in respect to implementation of this amendment within one year of its passage will deem all subsequent legislation passed by said Congress and future Congresses to be invalid until such responsibilities are enacted. This act cannot and shall not be modified in any way or struck down by the Supreme Court. Only a subsequent amendment to the Constitution can repeal or modify any portion of this amendment

APPENDIX B

Contrasting Liberal and Conservative Cultures

	Liberal	Conservative
Tribalism	One universal world mega-tribe with multiple classes	Small, multiple dynamic tribes
Classes	Static, based on birth and politics	Dynamic, based on talent for resource generation and distribution
	Basis of societal control	No societal control
The Leadership class	Duty to dominate lower classes for their own good	Duty to all of society
	Entitled to superior benefits	Egalitarian
Argumentation	Propaganda appealing to instinct	Logic and reasoning based on science and experience
Freedom	Willing to forgo freedom for security	Freedom is paramount

	Liberal	Conservative
Responsibility and Happiness	Government is responsible for everything	Individual is responsible for self, family, and tribe
	Government defines happiness	Individuals define their own happiness
Morality	Individuals are amoral	Individuals are moral
	The world tribe is moral	Tribes are amoral
Technology	Method for producing weapons for taking resources from others	Method for producing more necessities from available resources
Warfare, Conflict	Unnatural state between tribes; Natural state between classes	Natural state between tribes; No classes
	Class warfare is necessary to achieve cultural dominance and equal resource distribution	Violence and conflict between tribes is controlled by limited government
	Violence to individuals within a class is acceptable to achieve liberal goals	Violence to individuals within tribes is unacceptable and is immoral
Wealth	No distinction	A recognition of contribution to society
Resources		Property
Necessities		Food, lodging, etc.

	Liberal	Conservative
	A limited resource redistributed to achieve maximal political power	Not a physical necessity such as food or shelter, but a symbolic recognition of one's contributions to society
Resource Ownership	Resources belong to the entire world tribe	Private ownership by tribes (individuals, organizations, and companies)
Resource Conservation	Limited resources provided by nature	Resources are generated by tribes
	Must (re)distribute before they expire	Excess resources must be saved for future use
Resource Distribution	Goods and services distributed on basis of class, race, and political power	Goods and services distributed on the basis of the amount you contribute to society in the form of work

About the Author

The author was raised in the traditional American culture where you were encouraged to work for the things you needed and the extra treats you wanted. Taking government handouts was viewed as a weakness. He worked hard to achieve his goals and was on the honor roll in high school and graduated college with honors and with Phi Beta Kappa and Sigma Xi recognition of his academic achievements.

The author became concerned about the direction of the country when he saw the destruction and loss of life caused by the liberals with the bombing of Sterling Hall and the Kent State riots. The author feared that when the liberals realized that violence failed, they would switch to a devious and insidious but subtle approach to reshape US society. He experienced firsthand the attitudinal change that is leading to the liberal brainwashing of the US populace via the educational system. Their goal is to position the Ivy League liberals in control of the government.

He is fearful that the America he grew up in is being destroyed and decided to write a book explaining the common instincts of tribal society in American capitalism and socialist liberalism and why American capitalism supersedes European-style socialism. He is very concerned that the liberals will shut down debate on campuses and political rallies everywhere but will also violently attack people attending peaceful political and nonpolitical gatherings. They demonstrated such actions with the shooting of Rep. Steve Scalise at baseball practice. The author believes that such fascist actions are the result of the ancient primitive tribal instincts to kill and plunder their opponents, which pervades liberal socialism today, and, if not halted, the result can only lead to violent confrontations. He proposes an approach that will peacefully return the country to a true egalitarian democracy.